VIPASSANĀ : THE BUDDHIST WAY

VIPASSANĀ

THE BUDDHIST WAY

(The Based on Pāli Sources)

Edited by

Harcharan Singh Sobti

EASTERN BOOK LINKERS

DELHI : : (INDIA)

Published by :

EASTERN BOOK LINKERS

5825, New Chandrawal,
Jawahar Nagar, Delhi-110007
Ph. : 3970287
E-mail : easternbook@mantraonline.com

Edition : 2017

Price : 550.00

ISBN : 81-7854-52-2

Laser Type Setting :

CREATIVE GRAPHICS

Phone : 2195643

Printed at : R. K. Offset Process
Naveen Shahdara, Delhi-110032

DEDICATED

to

Kalyāna-mitta S.N. Goenka Ji

with reverence and gratitude.

PREFACE

When I attended a Seminar and *Vipassanā* Course during December 20, 1986 to January 1, 1987, of Vipassanā Research Institute, Dhammagiri at Igat Puri, (Nasik), under the guidance of *Kalyāna-mitta* S.N. Goenka ji, the Master used to refer to the verses of Gurū Nānak, occasionally, during his discourses. Once, I put this question to Goenka ji as to why does he quote Gurū Nānak while talking on *Vipassanā* ? His instant reply was that Gurū Nānak also practised *Vipassanā*. In this very meeting, Goenka Ji, very emphatically suggested that I should explore the Sources of *Vipassanā* in *Gurūbāṇi*. I propose to work on, as inspired by Goenka Ji, *The Path of Purification* (based on Sikh Scriptures). But, before that I wanted to explore the Sources of *Vipassanā* in Pāḷi literature.

I am greatly beholden to the contributers who provide theoretical frame-work of *Vipassanā*. Although, *Vipassanā* is a subject of practice, but, nonetheless, theory is one aspect of practice.

HARCHARAN SINGH SOBTI.

Id—Ul—Milad,
September, 22, 1991.
D13A/30, Model Town,
DELHI - 110009.

CONTENTS

I

Vipassanā : Sources in Pāḷi literature

S.K. Meshram

The dictionary meaning of the word *Vipassanā* is inward vision, insight, intuition or introspection.[1]

Thus, *Vipassanā* means to see things as they are : to see things in their true perspective, in their true nature. In other words, *Vipassanā* is a technique of self observation and the cultivation of such potentialities to perfection and the development of the precepts.

The primary source of our knowledge of *Vipassanā* meditation, we find in *Dhamma Cakka Pavattana Sutta* of *Saṃyutta Nikāya*.[2] and *Vinaya Mahāvaggo*.[3] While addressing the *Pañavaggiya Bhikkhus* in Migadāya Vana at Varaṇasī the Enlightened One, the Buddha said, 'There is a Middle Path, O Bhikkhus, avoiding these two extremes, discovered by the *Tathāgata* - a path which opens the eyes and bestows understanding, which leads to peace of mind, to the higher wisdom, to full Enlightenment, to Nibbāna. that is to say, *Sammā - Diṭṭhi, Sammā - Saṅkappo, Sammā - Vācā, Sammā - Kammanto, Sammā - Ājīvo, Sammā - Vāyāmo, Sammā - Sati, Sammā Samādhi.*

The Buddha excplained the Sammā samādhi in these words,"*Ya kho Bhikkhave cittassa ekaggatā - ayaṃ samādhi / cattāro satipaṭṭhānā Samādhi nimittā / Cattāro sammappadhāna Samādhi parikkhāra / Yā tesaṃ yeva dhammānaṃ āsevanā, bhāvanā, bahulikaranaṃ ayaṃ tattha samādhi bhāvanā* /.[4]

The meaning of the above passage is as follows :

"O Bhikkhus, whatever is one-pointedness of mind, this is concentration, the four arousings of mindfulness are the distinguishing marks of concentration, the four right efforts are the requisites for concentration. Whatever is the practice, the development, the increase of these very things, this is herein the development of concentration."

We find many references of *Vipassanā in* Tipiṭaka literature. In *Saṅgīti Sutta* of *Dīgha Nikāya* we are told -

" *Atthi Kho, āvuso, tena bhagavatā jānatā passatā arahatā sammāsambuddhena dve dhammā sammadakkhātā, tattha sabbeheva Samgāyitabbaṃ na vivaditabbaṃ, katame dve ?.... samatho ca vipassanā ca*".[5]

Its meaning is - "These are double doctrines, friends, which are perfectly set foth by the Exalted One, who knows, who sees. Thereon there should be a chanting in concord not in wrangling, that, thus this holy life may persist and be long maintained which are the doubles - calm and insight."

Majjhima Nikāya refers - "Monks, if a monk should wish, May I be agreeable to my fellows in the pure life, liked by them, revered and respected he should be one who fulfils the moral rules (*sīla*), who intends on calming the mind (*cetosamatha*) within, whose meditation (*Jhāna*) is uninterrupted, who is endowed with discerning (*Vipassanā*), a frequent of solitary abodes (*Suññāgāra*). [6]

The *Dasuttara Sutta* of *Dīgha Nikāya* says, "*Katame dve dhammā bhāvetabbā ? Samatho ca Vipassanā ca - ime dve Dhammā bhāvetabbā*". [7]

Which two things be practised ? Calm and Insight (meditation). These two things be practised.

The most important *Sutta* is *Satipaṭṭhāna Sutta* from *Majjhima Nikāya* which describes the applications of mindfulness as follows :-

"*Ekāyano ayaṃ bhikkhave, maggo sattānaṃ Visuddhiyā, sokaparidevānaṃ Samatikkamāya dukkha domanassānaṃ atthaṅgamāya ñāyassa adhigamāya nibbānassa sacchikiriyāya yadidaṃ cattāro satipaṭṭhānā.*" [8]

This is the only way, monks, for the purification of beings, for the overcoming of sorrow and misery, for the destruction of pain and grief, for gaining the knowledge, for attainment of *Nibbāna*, the four arousings of mindfulness.

Again in *Majjhima Nikāya Mahāvedalla Sutta* describes *Vipassanā*, as under -

"*Idhāvuso Saṁmā-diṭṭhi silanuggahitā ca hoti, suttanuggahitā ca hoti, sakachhā - nuggahitā ca hoti, samathānuggahitā ca hoti, Vipassanānuggahitā ca hoti.*" [9]

Here, friend, right understanding is forwarded by moral habits, and it is forwarded by hearing, and it is forwarded by discussion, and it is forwarded by calm and it is forwarded by vision.

Mahāgosiṅga Sutta from *Majjhima Nikāya* also refers *Vipassanā* in following words -

"*Idhāvuso Sāriputta, Bhikkhu paṭisallānārāmo hoti, Paṭisallamarato, ajjhattam cetosamathamanuyuttho anirākatajjhāno Vipassanāya samnnāgato*".[10]

Here, reverend Sāriputta, monk delighs in solitary meditation, he delighted by solitary meditation, he is intent on mental tranquillity within, his meditation is uninterrupted, he is endowed with vision, a cultivator of empty places.

Aṅguttara Nikāya also refers the word *Vipassanā* - "*dve bhikkhave dhammā, katame dve ? Samatho ca Vipassanā ca.*"[11]

O, monks there are two things : which two - calm and insight (meditation).

We find many references of *Vipassanā* Meditation in non-canonical literature also such as *Milinda - Pañho and Visuddhimagga*. In *Milinda - Pañho* it has been described thus - "*Āyasmā pi kho Nāgaseno Tassa Mahaupasikaya anumodanaṃ katvā attanā desitadhammaṃ paccavekkhamto Vipassanaṃ patthapetvā tasmiṃ yevāsane nisinno Sotāpatti phale patiṭṭhāsī*".[12]

The meaning of the above paragraph is thus - "And Nāgasena also, when he had concluded that thanks - giving discourse, felt the force of the truth he himself had preached and he too arrived at insight, he too entered, as he sat there upon the stream."

In *Samādhi Niddeso* of *Visuddhimaggo*, we find the word *Vipassanā* thus - " *Sekkha Puthujjanānaṃ Samāpattiyo Vutthaya samāhitena cittena vipassissamā" ti bhāvayattaṃ Vipassanāya padatthanatā appanāsamādhi bhāvanā pi sambadhe okāsādhiganaṃ yeva upacāra samādhibhāvanā pi vipassanānisaṃsā hoti*". [13]

Anussatikammaṭṭāna Niddeso refers the word in this way, "*Sallakkhanā ti vipassanā*". [14]

Observation is the insight.

Thus, in the above-mentioned paragraphs we have seen some of the sources of Vipassanā meditation traced in Tipiṭaka-Pāli literature and non-canonical literature.

Now we will see the aims and objectives of *Vipassanā*. It is very clear that the Buddha in his discourse has given the purpose of *Vipassanā* in the famous *Gāthā* of *Dhammapada*, which also contains the essence of *Dhamma*, the Buddha *Sāsana*. *Sabba Pāpassa akaranaṃ Kusalassa upasampadā sacitta pariyodapanaṃ etaṃ Buddhānasāsanaṃ*.[15]

Cease to do evil, learn to do good, cleanse your own heart, this is the teaching of the Buddhas.

Thus, it is very clear from the above *Gāthā* that the meditation or concentration of mind is a method of cleansing our hearts so that we can apprehend the truth and reality through serenity. Day and night, in sleeping, in awakening, our mind is always in turmoil of thoughts, emotions, desires, loves, hatreds, and worries. In such a condition of mind, right concentration of mind is very helpful.

In the words of John Walters we can put, "The Four Noble Truths, the three signs of Being, and other Buddhist Teaching which may have seemed puzzling are in the state of concentration, completely understood. All through this experience there is a feeling of light of gladness and of peace."[16]

In this way one can achieve Supreme Wisdom through *Vipassanā* meditation. While explaining the point very clearly John Walters said, "This road to Supreme Wisdom is reached in four stages of meditation or the four *Jhānas*. In the first stage the monk devotes his mind to reasoning on some religious subjects. In the second stage the monk's concentration gives his mind clarity and reason becomes replaced by pure intuition. Then in the third stage the subject of his thought and intuition fades away. Now the monk is filled with a sense of eternal joy. Lastly, in the fourth stage ecstasy passes, to be replaced by a purity of equanimity and mindfulness, devoid of either joy or sorrow. This indeed must be close to the peace of *Nibbāna*".[17]

There is no place for any kind of prayer in *Dhamma*. Instead, the concentration of mind through meditation and thereby reaching a comprehension of Reality, has important place in *Dhamma*. John Walters has explained this very clearly, " Formerly it was regarded as a useless pagan practice. But today methods of Buddhist meditation are studied by many Western psychologists. Some believe that it has strong therapeutic value. The concentration of all the mental faculties in meditation produces what is called 'onepointedness of mind'. In Right concentration the mind is devoted with intensity exclusively to a single object, thought or problem. Gradually his mental reaction to all outside stimulus disappears and he reaches a state of supreme serenity that can lead on into ecstasy and rapture. In such a state, the mind attains Transparent Clarity during which the truths, such as the nature of sorrow, are at last lucidly comprehended. Finally, in the concentration of a much practised and fully dedicated Buddhist, reason, emotions and feelings are lost in *Nibbāna*, the highest state of Enlightenment."[18]

Thus, " Meditational practices constitute the very core of the Buddhist approach to life", explains Edward Conze and further adds, "Enlightenment of the state of (Pāli : *Nibbāna*) *Nirvāṇa* is, of course, the ultimate aim of Buddhist meditation. On the way to *Nirvāṇa* they serve to promote spiritual development to diminish the impact of suffering, to calm the mind and to reveal the true facts of existence."[19]

"We have many people around us the whole day and there is noise everywhere. Hence it is very difficult to find peace of mind in daily life. Therefore those who have free time and who want to lead a secluded life can concentrate their minds in meditation. Instead of talking about faults or vices of other people one can think of meditation and practise it. This is better than sitting idle. This is possible in every-day llife.

In *Vipassanā paññā* will gradually develop and it will know things as they are. The *paññā* developed in *Vipassanā* is the 'Right Understanding' of the Eight fold Path which leads to *Nibbāna*.[20]

Nina Gorkan says, "I understand that in the development of *Vipassanā* we learn to see things as they are. Seeing things as they are means seeing *Nāma* and *Rūpa* as they are. So we should distinguish *Nāma* and *Rūpa* from each other more clearly. In *Vipassanā* we develop awareness. Awareness in Pāli is *Sati*."[21]

Thus, the aim of *Vipassanā* is detachment through the development of Wisdom. In other words, the development of *Paññā* which knows realities of life.

"The word *Samādhi* used in the Buddha *dhamma* means *Kusala cittassa ekaggatā*, the one-pointed state of the mind. When successfully practised it brings about the absence of wandering or distraction of mind, resulting in the accompanying states of calmness and serenity. It is in such a state of complete detachment and freedom from distraction that Wisdom dawns upon the individual. It is the state of Enlightenment or *Paññā*, the attainment of which is the ultimate goal of human life."[22]

He further adds, "*Sammā Samādhi* (Right Concentration) is the last state of the Noble Eight - fold Path, consists of exercises in concentration. The Buddhist monk is expected to devote some time of a day in the exercises of concentration of mind. Having divested the mind of all hindrances, the disciple in religion takes to contemplation, with unfailing regularity each day. As he progresses in his contemplation his mind begins to feel joy and his body becomes calm."[23]

The Buddha said, "*cattāto Bhikkhave Satipaṭṭhānā bhāvitā bahulīkatā ekamta - nibbidāya virāgāya nirodhāya upasamāya abhiññāya Sambodhāya nibbānāya samavattati.*"

"Brethren, these four foundations of mindfulness (*satipaṭṭāna*) when fully practised produce detachment, freedom from craving, complete release, perfect bliss, perfect wisdom, Enlightenment, *Nibbāna*."

To enter the practice of Insight Meditation (*Vipassanā*) means the cultivation of such potentialities to perfection and the developement of precepts, concentration and wisdom, from the lower to the higher levels. The precepts fall into two classes : Mundane consisting of the ordinary moral codes for laymen and *Bhikkhus*, and the Super mundane, which are developed only in persons practising Insight Meditation (*Vipassanā*) upto attainment of the Path. Concentration also falls into the same two classes, the mundane concentration of practitioners who have not yet attained to the levels of path and fruition and mundane concentration arising in persons practising Insight Meditation (*Vipassanā*) up to these levels.

The same applies to the faculty of wisdom, mundane wisdom comprising insight into what is meritorious or demeritorious, beneficial or detrimental, profitable or unprofitable and some understanding to the nature of mental and physical states and the three characteristics, while super mundane or developed wisdom arises in those practising Insight Meditation (*Vipassanā*) upto the levels of the path, the fruition and *Nibbāna*. [24]

Thus, by contemplating the object for *Vipassanā* or Insight, one can get rid of sufferings of rebirth, old age, disease and death. Moreover, the person practising meditation can attain the supreme state of emancipation called *Nibbāna*.

However, while studying the teachings and pondering over them, we must have clear understanding of our life. Moreover, if we were to develop *Vipassanā* without studying we could not understand what is the right path and what is wrong path. Without study of *Vipassanā* we cannot get right view of *Vipassanā* and *Samatha*.

Again, we should be very careful about the result of *Vipassanā*. Nina Gorkan has elaborated this important point well. She says, " We should not forget the Second Noble Truth - craving is the origin of *Dukkha*. As long as there is craving for *Nāma* and *Rūpa* there will be rebirth and thus no end of *Dukkha*. When people want to develop *Vipassanā* and they crave for results, they forget this Truth. For instance, they want to know within a short time the difference between seeing and colour, hearing and sound, they wish to experience the arising and falling away of

Nāma and *Rūpa*. But as long as they cling to obtain the result of *Vipassanā* there is no way that they will come to know the truth. The way of the Eight-fold Path is long, in order to become detached from the concept of self. *Paññā* has to know every kind of *Nāma* and *Rūpa* which appears. *Paññā* can only be developed through being mindful fo *Nāma* and *Rūpa* when they appear so that there will be precise knowledge of their different characteristics. [25]

Again, John Walters has cautioned the meditators in the following words, "But one should be very clear in his mind that the meditation is not a way to gain any kind of supernatural powers". He further adds, "The *Theravāda* Buddhism does not regard meditation or mind-training in general as a method of obtaining supernatural powers. It disapproves of self important people who claim that their meditation exercises have given them unearthly ecstasies or the ability to perform miracles or indeed any kind of conjuring trick." [26]

Those discerning persons who have joined in the practice should be considered as having done enormous benefit to themselves and to others, even including the nation, the faith and the Constitution.

"*Vuddhin virullim Vepullaṃ Pappoti Buddhasāsane*". "Finally, may you all be prosperous, flourishing and fortunate in *Dhamma*; in other words, may you attain the path, the fruition and *Nibbāna*." [27]

There are several benefits of practising Insight Meditation (*Vipassanā*). They are as follows :-

1. To give certainty into truth and not to be deceived by and not to hold fast to concepts (*paññatti*) which are mere mundane conventions.
2. To make people truly cultivated having good moral.
3. To make people love one another, make them feel their unity and to be compassionate towards each

other, and to make them have gladness and appreciation when they see others who are joyful.

4. To bring about a better standard of human behaviour.

5. To make people know themselves and how to govern themselves.

6. To cultivate humanity.

7. To bring about realisation of human unity.

8. To make people abide in gratitude.[28]

There are also some other benefits of *Vipassanā* meditation:

9. The destruction of defilements and the elimination of the ten fetters, means the cessation of suffering.

10. *Nibbāna* is the supreme object of Buddha's teaching. It is inconceivable, indescribable and unconditioned. It is the only object of the noble fruition state. One who attains the first state of sainthood gains the first vision of *Nibbāna*, thereby enjoying the taste of the bliss of *Nibbāna* by attaining the noble fruition state.

11. *Nirodhasamāpatti* means the cessation of perception of feeling and of the function of the mind in course of attainment.

12. After attaining the highest state of sainthood, the noble one becomes worthy of receiving gifts offered and homage paid by the world.[29]

We can sum up in the words of Alex Wayman, "All Buddhist sects granted the turths of Buddhism were discovered by the Buddha in the course of his meditation, especially beneath the Bodhi tree at Gaya in India. Thus, Meditation has a paramount role in Buddhism for indicating man's own ability to attain the truth." For further explanation he has quoted the *Visuddhimagga* and said, "Buddhaghosa arranged his *Visuddhimagga* in three parts in accordance with the Buddhist categories of three instructions that of morality for forming the basis of other two mental training aimed at *Samādhi* and insight leading to the seeing of things as they really are with full comprehension of Buddhist truth or discerning of reality".[30]

And as long as this strong belief is in the hearts of the laymen and the *Bhikkhus, Vipassanā* will be studied and practised all over the world.

References

1. Rhys Davids and William Stede, *Pāli-English Dictionary*, p. 627.
2. Bhikkhu Jagdish Kashyap, (Ed.) *Saṃyutta Nikāya* Vol. IV p. 360.
3. Bhikkhu Jagdish Kashyap (Ed.) *Vinaya (Mahāvagga)* Vol.1, p.13.
4. Bhikkhu Jagdish Kashyap (Ed.) *Majjhima Nikāya (Cullavedalla Sutta No. 44)* Vol. I, p. 371.
5. Bhikkhu Jagdish Kashyap (Ed.) *Dīgha Nikāya (Sangiti Sutta* No. 33) Vol. III, p. 169.
6. Bhikkhu Jagdish Kashyap (Ed.) *Majjhima Nikāya (Akaṅkheyya Sutta* No. 6) Vol. I, p. 44.
7. Bhikkhu Jagdish Kashyap (Ed.) *Dīgha Nikāya (Dasuttara Sutta* No. 34) Vol. III p. 211.
8. Bhikkhu Jagdish Kashyap (Ed.) *Majjhima Nikāya* (*Satti Paṭṭhāna Sutta No.10*) Vol. I, p. 76.
9. Bhikkhu Jagdish Kashyap (Ed.) *Majjihima Nikāya* (*Mahāvedalla Sutta No* 43) Vol. I, p. 362.
10. Bhikkhu Jagdish Kashyap (Ed.) *Majjhima Nikāya* (*Mahāgosinga* Sutta No. 32) Vol. I, p. 264.
11. Bhikkhu Jagdish Kashyap (Ed.) *Aṅguttara Nikāya* (*Samāpattivaggo*) Vol. I, p.87.
12. R.D. Wadekar *Milinda Pañho* p. 14.
13. Revatadhamma (Ed.) *Visuddhimagga* Part II, 806-807.

14. D.D. Kosambi, *Vissuddhimagga p. 256.*
15. *Dhammapada Gāthā* No. 183.
16. John Walters, *Mind Unshaken p. 85.*
17. *Ibid* p. 19
18. *Ibid* p. 38
19. *Ibid* p. 90
20. Gorkan Nina Van *Buddhism in Daily Life* pp. 20-21.
21. *Ibid* p. 117
22. Bhahadur Mal, *The Religion of Buddha*. pp. 146-147
23. *Ibid* p. 145
24. *Ibid* p. 13
25. Gorkan Nina Van *op. cit* p.154
26. John Walters *op.cit* p. 93
27. Ven. Tepasiddhi Muni Mahathera, *The Path to Nibbāna* p.15.
28. *Ibid* p. 36
29. Edward Conze, *Buddhist Meditation* p.41.
30. Alex Wayman, *Buddhist Insigtht p.69.*

II

Mahā Satipaṭṭhāna Sutta[1]

Translated by

T.W. and C.A.F. Rhys Davids

Thus have I heard.

I. The Exalted One was once staying among the Kurus. Kammassadhamma is a city of the Kuru country. There the Exalted One addressed the brethren, saying, '*Bhikkhus* !' 'Reverend sir !' responded the brethren. And the Exalted One said :

The one and only path, *Bhikkhus* leading to the purification of beings, to passing far beyond grief and lamentation, to the dying-out of ill and misery, to the attainment of right method[2]; to the realization of *Nibbāna* is that of the Fourfold Setting up of Mindfulness.

Which are the Four ? Herein[3], O *Bhikkhus* let a brother, as to the body, continue so to look upon the body that he remains ardent, self-possessed, and mindful, having overcome both the hankering and the dejection common in the world. And in the same way as to feelings, thoughts and ideas, let him so look upon each, that he remains ardent, self-possessed, and mindful, having overcome both the hankering and the dejection common in the world.

2. And how, *Bhikkhus,* does a brother so continue to consider the body ?

Herein.[4] O *Bhikkhus,* let a brother, going into the forest, or to the roots of a tree, or to an empty chamber, sit down cross-legged, holding the body erect, and set his mindfulness alert.[5]

Mindful let him inhale, mindful let him exhale. Whether he inhales a long breath, let him be conscious thereof; or whether he exhales a long breath, let him be conscious thereof. Whether he inhales a short breath, or exhales a short breath, let him be conscious thereof. Let him practice with the thought 'Conscious of my whole body will I exhale.' Let him practice with the thought 'I will inhale tranquillizing my bodily organism'; let him practise with the thought 'I will exhale tranquillizing my bodily orgainsim.'

Even as a skilful turner, or turner's apprentice, drawing (his string) out at length, or drawing it out short, is conscious that he is doing one or the other, so let a brother practise inhaling and exhaling.

So does he, as to the body, continue to consider the body, either internally or externally, or both internally and externally. He keeps on considering how the body is something that comes to be, or again he keeps on considering how the body is something that passes away; or again he keeps on considering the coming to be with the passing away; or again, conscious that 'There is the body, mindfulness hereof becomes thereby established, far enough for the purposes of knowledge and of self-collectedness. And he abides independent, grasping after nothing in the world whatever. Thus, *Bhikkhus*, does a brother continue to regard the body.

3. And moreover, *Bhikkhus*, a brother when he is walking, is aware of it thus :- 'I walk' ; or when he is standing, or sitting, or lying down, he is aware of it. However he is disposing the body, he is aware thereof.

So does he, as to the body, continue to consider the body, either internally or externally, or both internally and externally. He keeps on considering how the body is something that comes to be, or again he keeps on considering how the body is something that passes away ;

or again he keeps on considering the coming to be with the passing away; or again, conscious that 'There is the body', mindfulness hereof becomes thereby established, far enough for the purposes of knowledge and of self-collectedness. And he abides independent, grasping after nothing in the world whatever. Thus, *Bhikkhus,* does a brother continue to regard the body.

4. And moreover, *Bhikkhus*, a brother - whether he departs or returns, whether he looks at or looks away from, whether he has drawn in or stretched out [his limbs], whether he has donned under-robe, over-robe, or bowl, whether he is eating, drinking, chewing, reposing, or whether he is obeying the calls of nature - is aware of what he is about. In going, standing, sitting, sleeping, watching, talking, or keeping silence, he knows what he is doing.

So does he, as to the body, continue to consider the body, either internally or externally, or both internally and externally. He keeps on considering how the body is something that comes to be, or again he keeps on considering how the body is something that passes away : or again he keeps on considering the coming to be with the passing away; or again, conscious that 'There is the body', mindfulness hereof becomes thereby established, far enough for the purposes of knowledge and of self-collectedness. And he abides independent, grasping after nothing in the world whatever. Thus, *Bhikkhus*, does a brother continue to consider the body.

5. And moreover, *Bhikkhus*, a brother reflects upon this very body, from the soles of his feet below upward to the crown of his head, as something enclosed in skin and full of divers impurities : - 'Here is in this body hair and down, nails, teeth, skin, flesh, sinews, bones, marrow, kidney, heart, liver, membranes, spleen, lungs, stomach, bowels, intestines; excrement, bile, phlegm, pus, blood, sweat, fat, tears, serum, saliva, mucus, synovic fluid, urine'.

Just as if there were a double-mouthed sample-bag[6], *Bhikkhus*, full of various sorts of grain, such as rice, paddy, beans, vetches, sesamum or rice husked for boiling; and a keen-eyed man were to reflect as he poured them out :- 'That's rice, that's paddy, those are beans,' and so forth. Even so, *Bhikkhus*, does a brother reflect upon the body, from the soles of the feet below upward to the crown of the head, as something enclosed in skin and full of divers impurities.

So does he, as to the body, continue to consider the body, either internally or externally, or both internally and externally. He keeps on considering how the body is something that comes to be, or again he keeps on considering how the body is something that passes away; or again he keeps on considering the coming to be with the passing away; or again, conscious that 'There is the body', mindfulness hereof becomes thereby established, far enough for the purposes of knowledge and of self-collectedness. And he abides independent, grasping after nothing in the world whatever. Thus *Bhikkhus*, does a brother continue to regard the body.

6. And moreover, *Bhikkhus*, a brother reflects upon this very body, however it be placed or disposed, with respect to its fundamentals : - 'There are in this body the four primary elements of earth, water, heat, and air.' Just as a cattle-butcher, or his apprentice, when he has slain an ox, displays the carcase piecemeal at the crossways as he sits, evern so, *Bhikkhus,* does a brother reflect upon this very body... with respect to its fundamental constituents...

So does he, as to the body, continue to consider the body, either internally or externally, or both internally and externally. He keeps on considering how the body is something that comes to be, or again he keeps on considering how the body is something that passes away ; or again he keeps on considering the coming to be with the passing away; or again, conscious that 'There is the body', mindfulness hereof becomes thereby established, far enough for the purposes of knowledge and of self-collectedness. And he abides independent, grasping after nothing in the world whatever. Thus *Bhikkhus*, does a brother continue to regard the body.

7. And moreover, *Bhikkhus,* a brother, just as if he had seen a body abandoned in the charnel-field, dead for one, two, or three days, swollen, turning black and blue, and decomposed, applies that perception to this very body (of his own), reflecting : 'This body, too is even so constituted, is of even such a nature, has not got beyond that (fate).'

So does he, as to the body, continue to consider the body, either internally or externally, or both internally and externally. He keeps on considering how the body is something that passes away; or again he keeps on considering the coming to be with the passing away; or again, conscious that 'There is the body', mindfulness hereof becomes thereby established, far enough for the purposes of knowledge and of self-collectedness. And he abides independent, grasping after nothing in the world whatever. Thus *Bhikkhus,* does a brother continue to regard thebody.

8. And moreover, *Bhikkhus*, a borther, just as if he had seen a body abandoned in the charnel-field pecked by crows, ravens, or vultures, gnawn by dogs or jackals or by various small creatures, applies that perception to this very bodv (of his own), reflecting : 'This body, too, is even so constituted, is of such a nature, has not got beyond that (fate).'

So does he, as to the body, continue to consider the body, either internally or externally, or both internally and externally. He keeps on considering how the body is something that comes to be, or again he keeps on considering how the body is something that passes away ; or again he keeps on considering the coming to be with the passing away ; or again, conscious that 'There is the body', mindfulness hereof becomes thereby established, far enough for the purposes of knowledge and of sel-collectedness. And he abides independent grasping after nothing in the world whatever. Thus, *Bhikkhus*, does a brother continue to regard the body.

9. And moreover, *Bhikkhus*, a brother, just as if he had seen a body abandoned in the charnel-field [reduced to] a chain of bones hanging together by tendons, with flesh and blood yet about it, or stripped of flesh but yet spotted with blood; or cleaned of both flesh and blood; or reduced to bare bones, loosed from tendons, scattered here and there, so that the bones of a hand lie in one direction, in another those of a leg, in another the pelvis, in another the spinal vertebrae, in another the skull, applies that perception to this very body (of his own) reflecting : 'This body, too, is even so constituted, is of such a nature, has not got beyond that (fate).'

So does he, as to the body, continue to consider the body, either internally or externally, or both internally and externally. He keeps on considering how the body is something that comes to be, or again he keeps on considering how the body is something that passes away; or again he keeps on considering the coming to be with the passing away; or again, conscious that 'There is the body', mindfulness hereof becomes thereby established, far enough for the purposes of knowledge and of self-collectedncess. And he abides independent, grasping after nothing in the world whatever. Thus, *Bhikkhus,* does a brother continue to regard the body.

10. And moreover, *Bhikkhus*, a brother, just as if he had seen a body abandoned in the charnel-field, [reduced] white bones the colour of a sea-shell ... or to a mere heap of bones a year old ... or to rotten powder, this perception does he apply to this very body (of his own) reflecting : - 'This body too is even so constituted, is of such a nature, has not got beyond that (fate).'

So does he, as to the body, continue to consider the body, either internally or externally, or both internally and externally. He keeps on considering how the body is something that comes to be, or again he keeps on considering how the body is something that passes away; or again he keeps on considering the coming to be with the passing away; or again conscious that 'There is the body', and mindfulness hereof becomes thereby established, far enough for the purposes of knowledge and of self-collectedness. And he abides independent, grasping after nothing in the world whatever. Thus *Bhikkhus*, does a brother, as to the body, continue to consider the body.

11. And how, *Bhikkhus*, does a brother as to the feelings, continue to consider the feelings ?

Herein, O *Bhikkhus*, is a brother when affected by a feeling of pleasure, aware of it, reflecting : 'I feel a pleasureable feeling.' So, too, is he aware when affected by a painful feeling, or by a neutral feeling, or by a pleasant or painful or neutral feeling concerning material things, or by a pleasant or painful or neutral feeling concerning spiritual things.

So does he, as to the feelings, continue to consider feeling, both internally and externally, or internally and externally together. He keeps on considering how the feelings are something that comes to be, or again he keeps on considering how the feelings are something that passes away, or he keeps on considering their coming to be with their passing away; Or again, with the consciousness: 'There is feeling', mindfulness thereof becomes thereby established far enough for the purposes of knowledge and of self collectedness. And he abides independent, grasping after nothing in the world whatever. Thus, *Bhikkhus,* does a borther, with respect to the feelings, continue to consider feeling.

12. And how, *Bhikkhus*, does a brother, as to thought, continue to consider thought [7]?

Herien, O *Bhikkhus*, a brother, if his thought be lustful, is aware that it is so, or if his thought be free from lust, is aware that it is so; or if his thought be full of hate, or free from hate, or dull, or intelligent, or attentive, or distrait, or exalted, or not exalted, or mediocre, or ideal, or composed, or discomposed, or liberated, or bound, he is aware in each case that his thought is so, reflecting : 'My thought is lustful', and so on.

So does he, as to thought, continue to consider thought, internally or externally, or internally and externally together. He keeps on considering how thought is something that comes to be, or again he keeps on considering how a thought is something that passes away, or again he ever considers its coming to be and passing away together. Or again, with the consciousness : 'There is a thought', mindfulness thereof becomes thereby established, far enough for the purposes of knowledge and of self-possession. And he abides independent, grasping after nothing in the world whatever. Thus, *Bhikkhus*, does a brother, with respect to thought, continue to consider thought.

13. And how, *Bhikkhus*, does a brother, as to ideas[8] continue to consider ideas ?

Herein, O *Bhikkhus*, a brother, as to ideas, continues to consider ideas from the point of view of the Five Hindrances.

And how, *Bhikkhus*, does a brother, as to ideas, continue to consider ideas relating to the Five Hindrances?

Herein, O *Bhikkhus*, a brother, when within him is sensuous desire, is aware of it, reflecting : 'I have within me sensuous desire.' Or again, when within him is no sensuous desire, he is aware of this. And he knows of the uprising of such desire unfelt before, knows too of his putting aside that uprisen sensuous desire, knows too of the non-arising in future of that banished sensuous desire.

[The paragraph is repeated of ill-will, sloth and torpor, flurry and worry, and doubt.]

So does he, as to ideas, continue to consider them, both internally or externally, or internally and externally together. He ever considers how an idea is a thing that comes to be, again he ever considers how an idea is a thing that passes away, or he ever considers their coming to be with their passing away; or again, with the consciousness : 'There is such and such an idea,' mindfulness thereof is thereby established, far enough for purposes of knowledge and of self-possession. And he abides independent, grasping after nothing in the world whatever. Thus, *Bhikkhus* does a brother, with respect to dispositions, continue to consider dispositions in the case of the Five Hindrances.

14. And moreover, Bhikkhus, a brother, as to ideas, continues to consider these from the point of view of the Five *Skandhas* of Grasping. And how, *Bhikkhus*, does he so consider them ?

Herein, O *Bhikkhus*, a brother reflect : 'Such is material form, such is its genesis, such its passing away; such is feeling - perception - the mental activities - such is cognition, its genesis, its passing away.

So does he, as to dispositions, continue to consider them, ...

15. And moreover, *Bhikkhus*, a brother, as to ideas, continues to consider ideas from the point of view of the Six Internal and External Spheres of Sense. And how does he do this ?

Herein, O *Bhikkhus*, a brother, is aware of the organ of sight, is aware of the objects of sight, and any Fetter which arises on account of them both - of that, too, is he aware ; and how there comes an uprising of a Fetter non arisen before - of that, too, is he aware ; and how there comes a putting aside of a Fetter that has arisen of that, too, is he aware ; and how in the future there shall arise no Fetter that has been put aside- of that, too, is he aware.

And so, too, with respect to the organ of hearing and sounds, to the organ of smell and odours, to the organ of taste and tastes, to the organ of touch and tangibles, to the sensorium and images, he is aware of the sense and of the object, of any Fetter which arises on account of both, of how there comes an uprising of a Fetter not arisen before, of how there comes a putting-aside of a Fetter that has arisen, and of how in the future there shall arise no Fetter that has been put aside.

So does he, as to ideas, continue to consider ideas, from the point of view of the Six internal and External Spheres of Sense.

16. And moreover, *Bhikkhus*, a brother, as to ideas, continues to consider ideas, with respect to the Seven Factors of Enlightenment. And how does he do this ?

Herein, O *Bhikkhus*, a brother, if there be present to him subjectively mindfulness as a factor fo enlightenment, is aware that it is present. Or if it be absent, he is subjectively aware of its absence. And how there comes an uprising of such mindfulness not hitherto uprisen - of that, too, is he aware ; and how there comes a full development of such mindfulness when it has arisen - of that too is he aware. And so too with respect to the other subjective factors of enlightenment : - search the truth, energy, joy, serenity, rapture, equanimity - he is aware if they are subjectively present, or absent, and he is aware of how there comes an uprising of any factor not hitherto uprisen, and of how there comes a full development of such factors when it has arisen.

So does he, as to ideas, continue to consider ideas from the point of view of the Seven Factors of Enlightenment

17. And moreover, *Bhikkhus*, a brother, as to ideas, continues to consider ideas from the point of view of the Four Aryan Truths. And how does he do this ?

Herein, O *Bhikkhus*, a brother at the thought : 'This is ill !' is aware of it as it really is : - at the thought : 'This is the coming to be of Ill !" is aware of it as it really is : - at the thought : 'This is the cessation of Ill!' is aware of it as it really is :- at the thoutght : 'This is the way leading to the cessation of Ill !' is aware of it as it really is.

18. And what, *Bhikkhus*, is the Aryan truth [regarding] Ill?

Birth is painful, old age is painful[10] death is painful, grief, lamentation,suffering, misery and despair are painful, painful is it not to get what is wished for, in a word, the Five Groups that arise from Grasping are connected with pain.[11]

And what, *Bhikkhus*, is birth ? Birth is the production, the outcome[12] the rising up in a new form, the appearance of the Groups, the acquisition of sense spheres, by this or that being in this or that class of beings. This is what is called birth.

And what, *Bhikkhus*, is growing old[13]? Growing old is the decay, the decrepitude, the breaking-up, the hoariness, the wrinkled state, the shrinkage of life's span, the collapse[14] of the sense-faculties of this or that being in this or that class of beings. This is what is called growing old.

And what, *Bhikkhus*, is dying ?

Dying is the fall (out of any state), the dropping out of it, the dissolution, the disappearance, the death, the dying, the accomplishment of the life-term, the breaking up of the Groups, the laying down of the body of this or that being in this or that class of beings. This is called dying.

And what, *Bhikkhus*, is grief ?

Grieving is the state of woe, heart ache, and affliction. The inward grief, the hidden wretchedness, of one who is visited by some calamity or other, of one who is smitten by some kind of ill. This is what is called grief.

And what, *Bhikkhus*, is lamenting ?

Lamenting is the act and the state of mourning, lamentation, deploring, of one who is visited by some calamity or other, of one who is smitten by some kind of ill. This is what is called lamenting.

And what, *Bhikkhus*, is suffering ?

Suffering is bodily ill, bodily pain, ill that is born of bodily contact, the being bodily affected by what is painful. This is what is called suffering.

And what, *Bhikkhus*, is misery ?

Misery is mental ill, mental pain, ill that is born of mental contact, the being mentally affected by what is painful. This is what is called misery.

And what, *Bhikkhus*, is despair ?

Despair is the act and state of dejection, of despondency, of one who is visited by some calamity or other, of one who is smitten by some kind of ill. This is what is called despair.

And what, *Bhikkhus*, is the ill of not getting what is wished for ?

In beings subject to birth the wish arises : - 'Ah ! if only we were not subject to birth, if only we could avoid being born !' But this is not to be got by wishing. This is the ill of not getting what is wished for. So too in the case of growing old, falling ill, dying, grieving, lamenting, suffering, being in misery and in despair, in being subject to these the wish arises :- 'Ah ! if only we were not subject to this one or that one of those things ! If only we could avoid them !' But this cannot be had for the wishing. This again is the ill of not getting what is wished for.

And what, *Bhikkhus*, is 'in a word the Five Groups that arise from Grasping'? These are the Groups of materials form, of feeling, of perception, of dispositions, and of cognition that arise from grasping. This is what is called 'in a word the Five groups that arise from Grasping are associated with Ill.'

This, *Bhikkhus*, is the Aryan Truth regarding Ill.

19. And what, *Bhikkhus*, is the Aryan Truth concering the coming to be of Ill ?

Even this Craving, potent for rebirth, that is accompanied by lust and self-indulgence, seeking satisfaction now here now there, to wit, the craving for the life of sense, the craving for becoming (renewed life), and the craving for not becoming (for no rebirth).[15]

Now this Craving, *Bhikkhus*, where does it take its rise, where does it have its dwelling ? In those material things of this world which are dear to us, which are pleasant. There does Craving take its rise, there does it dwell.

What things in this world are dear, what things are pleasant ? The sense of sight, the sense of hearing, the senses of smell, taste, touch and imagination - these are the things in this world that are dear, that are pleasnt. There does Craving take its rise, there does it dwell.

The thoughts that arise through sight, the thoughts that arise through hearing, the thoughts that arise through smell, taste, touch and imagination - these are the things in this world that are dear, that are pleasant. There does Craving take its rise, there does it dwell.

The stimulus of visual sense, the stimulus of auditory sense, the stimulus of the senses of smell, taste, touch and imagination - these are the things in this world that are dear, that are pleasant. There does Craving take it rise, there does it dwell.

Feeling that is born of the stimulus of the visual sense, feeling that is born of the stimulus of the auditory sense, feeling that is born of the stimulus of the senses of smell, taste, touch and feeling born of imagination - these are the things in this world that are dear, that are pleasant. There does Craving take its rise, there does it dwell.

The perceiving of things visible, the perceiving of things audible, the perceiving of things odorous, sapid, tangible, of things in memory recalled - these are the things in this world that are dear, that are pleasant. There does Craving take its rise, there does it dwell.

Intention concerned with things visible, intentions concerned with things audible, intentions concerned with things odorous, sapid, that may be smelt, tasted touched, tangible, with things in memory recalled - these are the things in this world that are dear, that are pleasnt. There does Craving take its rise, there does it dwell.

Craving for things visible, craving for things audible, craving for things that may be smelt, tasted, touched, for things in memory recalled - these are the things in this world that are dear, that are pleasant. There does Craving take its rise, there does it dwell.

Pre-occupation about things seen, pre-occupation about things heard, pre-occupation about things smelt, tasted, tangible, about things in memory recalled — these are the things in this world that are dear, that are pleasant. There does Craving take its rise, there does it dwell.

Deliberating about things seen, deliberating about things heard, deliberating about things smelt, tasted, tangible, about things in memory recalled - these are the things in this world that are dear, that are pleasant. And there does Craving take its rise, there does it dwell.

This, *Bhikkhus*, is what is called the Aryan Truth concerning the coming to be of Ill.

20. And what, *Bhikkhus*, is the Aryan Truth concerning the cessation of Ill ?

The utter cessation of and disenchantment about that very Craving, giving it up, renouncing it, emancipation from it, detachment from it.

But now this Craving, *Bhikkhus*, where, in being put

away, is it put away; where, in ceasing, does it cease ? In those material things of this world which are pleasant - there may this Craving be put away, there does it cease.

What things in this world are dear, what things are pleasant? The sense of sight, the sense of hearing, the senses of smell, taste, touch and imagination - these are the things in this world that are dear, that are pleasant. Here may this Craving be put away, here does it cease.

Things seen, things heard, things smelt, tasted, tangible, things in memory recalled - these are the things in this world that are dear, that are pleasant. Here may this Craving be put away, here does it cease.

The thoughts that arise through sight, the thoughts that arise through hearing, the thoughts that arise through smell, taste, touch and imagination - these are the things in this world then are dear, that are pleasnt. Here may this Craving be put away, here does it cease.

The stimulus of visual sense, the stimulus of auditory sense, the stimulus of the senses of smell, taste, touch and imagination - these the things in this world that are dear, that are plesant. Here may this Craving be put away, here does it cease.

Feeling that is born of the stimulus of the visual sense, feeling that is born of the stimulus of the auditory sense, feeling then is born of the stimulus of the senses of smell, taste touch and feeling born of imagination - these are the things in this world that are dear, that are pleasant. Here may this Craving be put away, here does it cease.

The perceiving of things visible, the perceiving of things audible, the perceiving of things odorous, sapid, tangible, of things in memory recalled - these are the things in this world that all dear, here does it cease.

Intentions concerned with things visible, intentions concerned with things intentions concerned with things odorous, sapid at may be smelt, tasted, touched, tangible, with things in memory recalled - these are the things in this world that are dear, that are pleasant. Here may this Craving be put away, here does it cease.

Craving for things visible, craving for things audible, craving for things that may be smelt, tasted, touched, for things in memory recalled - these are the things in this world that are dear, that are pleasnt. Here may this Craving be put away, here does it cease.

Pre-occupation about things seen, pre-occupation about things heard, pre-occupation about things smelt, tasted, tangible, about things in memory recalled - these are the things in this world that are dear, that are pleasnt, Here may this Craving he put away, here does it cease.

Deliberating about things seen, deliberating about things heard, deliberating about things smelt, tasted, tangible, about things in memory recalled - these are the things in this world that are dear, that are pleasant. Here may Craving be put away, here does it cease.

This, *Bhikkhus*, is what called the Aryan Truth concerning the cessation of Ill.

21. And what, bhikkhu is the Aryan Truth concerning the Way that leads to the Cessation of Ill ?

This is that Aryan Eightfold Path, to wit, right view, right aspiration, right speech, right doing, right livelihood, right efforts, right mindfulness, right rapture.

And what, *Bhikkhus*, is right view ?

Knowledge, *Bhikkhus*, about Ill, knowledge about the coming to be of Ill, knowledge about the cessation of Ill, knowledge about the Way that leads to the cessation of Ill. This is what is called right view.

And what, *Bhikkhus*, is right aspiration ?

This aspiration towards renunciation[16], the aspiration towards benevolence, the aspiration towards kindness. This is what is called right aspiration.

And what, *Bhikkhus*, is right speech ?

Abstaining from lying, slander, abuse and idle talk. This is what is called right speech.

And what, *Bhikkhus*, is right doing ?

Abstaining from taking life, from taking what is not given, from carnal indulgence. This is what is called right doing.

And what, *Bhikkhus*, is right livelihood?

Herein, O Bhikkhus, the Aryan disciple having put away wrong livelihood, supports himself by right livelihood.

And What, *Bhikkhus*, is right effort ?

Herien, O *Bhikkhus*, a brother makes effort in bringing forth will that evil and bad states that have not arisen within him may not arise, to that end he stirs up energy, he grips and forces his mind. That he may put away evil and bad states that have arisen within him he puts forth will, he makes effort, he stirs up energy, he grips and forces his mind that good states which have not arisen may arise he puts forth will, he makes effort, he stirs up energy, he grips and forces his mind. This is what is called right effort.

And What, *Bhikkhus*, is righ mindfulness ?

Herein, O *Bhikkhus*, a brother, as to the body, continues so to look upon the body, that he remains ardent, self possessed and mindful, having overcome both the hankering and the dejection common in the world. And in the same way as to feelings, thoughts and ideas, he so looks upon each, that he remains ardent, self-possessed and mindful, having overcome the hankering and the dejection that is common in the world. This is what is called right mindfulness.

And what, *Bhikkhus*, is right rapture ?

Herein, O *Bhikkhus*, a brother, aloof from sensuous appetites, aloof from evil ideas, enters into and abides in the First *Jhāna* wherein there is cogitation and deliberation, which is born of solitude and is full of joy and ease. Suppressing cogitation and deliberation, he enters into and abides in the Second *Jhāna*, which is self-evoked, born of concentation, full of joy and ease, in that, set free from cogitation and deliberation, the mind grows calm and sure, dwelling on high. And further, disenchanted with joy, he abides calmly contemplative while, mindful and self-possessed, he feels in his body that ease whereof Aryans declare 'He that is calmly contemplative and aware, he dwelleth at ease.' So does he enter into and abide in the Third *Jhāna*. And further, by putting aside ease and by putting aside malaise, by the passing away of the happiness and of the melancholy he used to feel, he enters into and abides in the Foruth *Jhāna*, raputre of utter purity of mindfulness and eqanimity, wherin neither ease is felt nor any ill. This is what is called right rapture.

This, *Bhikkhus*, is the Aryan Truth concerning the Way leading to the cessation of Ill.

So does he, with respect to ideas continue to consider ideas, both internally, or externally, or internally and externally toghether. He ever considers how ideas are something that comes to be, again he ever considers how they are something that passes away, or again with the consciousness 'There are ideas,' maindfulness thereof is therby established, far enough for pursposes of knowledge and of self-possession. And he abides independent, grasping after nothing in the world whatever. Thus, *Bhikkhus*, does a brother, with respect to ideas, continue to consider ideas with respect to the Four Aryan Truths.

22. *Bhikkhus* ! whoso shall thus pracitse these Four Application of Mindfulness for seven years, in him one or two kinds of fuition may be looked for :- either in this

present life The Knowledge [17] or if there be yet residuum for rebirth, the state of him who returns no more. Or, not to speak of seven years, *Bhikkhus*, whoso shall thus pracitse these Four for six years, for five only, for four only, for three only, for two only, for one year only, in him one or two kinds of fruition may be looked for : either in this present life The Knwledge, or, if there be yet reisiduum for rebirth, the state of him who returns no more. Or not to speak of one year, *Bhikkhus*, whose shall thus practise these Four for six months, or for five months, for four only, or three, or two, or one month only, or half a month only, in him one or two kinds of fruition may be looked for : either in this present life The Knowledge, or, if there by yet residuum for rebirth, the state of him who returns no more. Or not to speak of half a month, *Bhikkhus,* whoso shall thus practise these four for seven days, in him one of two kinds of fruition may be looked for : either in this present life The Knowledge, or if there be yet residuum for rebrith, the state of him who returns no more. It was on account of this that that was said which was said (at the beginning) 'The one and only path *Bhikkhus*, leading to the purification of beings, to passing far beyond grief and lamentation, to the dying out of ill and misey, to the attainment of tight method, to the realization of *Nibbāna* is that of the Four-fold Setting-up of Starting.

Thus spake the Exalted One. Pleased were the brethren, delighting in that which was spoken by the Exalted One.

Notes and References

1. *Dīgha Nikāya* (*Sutta No.* 22) Vol. II pp. 291-315 T.W. and C.A.F. Rhys Davids (Trs.) *Dialogues of the Buddha* (Translation of *Dīgha Nikāya*) S.B.B. Vol. III Part II pp. 327-346.

2. Ñāya Practical Buddhism is summed up (*Majjhima N*. Vol I, pp 181, 197) as exertion in *ñāya, dhamma*, and *kusala* (the Method, the Norm, and the Good). Ñāya is defined at *Saṃyutta* V, 388 as what comes pretty much to our method in philosophy. Above (p. 167) it is rendered System. There, in a very old verse, the Buddha says that seeking after Good he had been a pilgrim through the realm of System and Law, outside of which no victory can be won.

3. The commentarial tradition sees in this word *idha*, the implication of 'belonging to this order or doctrine or school' *(imasmiṁsāsane)*, and thus an antithesis to '*ito bahiddhā*,' outside this [order] - an expression which occurs immediatly after the verse mentioned in the last note.

4. Quoted *Patisambhidā* I, 175, and '*Yogāvacara Manual,*' p.1. Each quotation gives a word for word commentary ; and so does Sum. I, 210.

5. *Primukham satim upatthapati,* literally, 'set up his memory in face of (the obejct of his thought). The ultimate object is throughout, as the '*Yogāvacara Manual*' says, *Nirvāṇa*. Examples of the subsidiary, changing, objects of thought are given in what follows.

6. Mutoli. Buddhaghosa has no explanation 'But

Daramitipola says *mallak pasumbiyak,* that is, a small bag, such as is used by grain merchants for keeping samples in. The practicular kind meant is kept tied up with string at both ends, and either end can be opened. The word only occurs in this connexion (here. and at M.I, 57; III, 90) The spelling of the word is uncertain.

7. *Citta.* The reader is reminded that 'Thought' is used here for *citta* in the widest sense possible to that term, such as is intended when, in the Christian tradition, it is made to complement the 'word and deed' of the Epistles. And as such it is 'thinking' rather than 'what is thought', that should be understood.

8. *Dhammā.*

9. What follows (down to the line and space on *Majjhima Nikāya* vol. I pp. 55-56.) is not found in the *Majjhima* recension of the *Satipaṭṭhāna*. Except for this the two recensions agree, and ours here is dobtless called the *Mahā Satipaṭṭhāna,* precisely because, to that extent, it is longer. That would show that when that title was first used the *Majjhima* recension was already known. It would not follow that the *Dīgha* is younger than the *Majjhima;* they may have been edited at the same time from older material.

   The *Dīgha* addition is interesting as containing a fragment of Old commentary (as old as the texts) of which other fragments are found in the *Nikāyas,* and also in the *Vinaya.*

   The *Vibhaṅga* (99-106) quotes this *Dīgha* addition verbatim.

10. Many Mss. And the Colombo edition of 1876 add 'disease is painful.' But this is not mentioned in the word-for-word commentary that follows. It is probably transferred as a gloss from the *Saṃyutta*

recentsion of the Four Truths (*Saṃyutta Nikāya* Vol. I, p. 421) which differs slightly from that of the repeaters of the *Digha* (the *Digha bhānkā*).

11. *Pañca 'upādānakkhandhā*. The groups are the five groups of material and mental qualities that form, in combination brought about by grasping, an individual. One might, therefore, express this central thought of the first Aryan truth in modern Western language by saying that pain is involved in individuality a most pregnant and far reaching suggestion. The rest of the Truth is merely a statement of facts universally adimtted.

12. *Sañjāti* only found elsewhere as yet *Digh* I, 227, where it means the produce arising out of an estate an accruing to the landlord.

13. Cf. *Dhammasaṅgani* and Bud. Psy. on *rūpassa jaratā*.

14. *Paripāka*, which in all other passages means maturity, must here mean over-ripeness, loss of power through having reached their full vigour and begun to give out.

15. *Vibhava*. This word usually means power, prosperity, success - the prefix vi being used as an intensitive particle. In this particular connexion the traditional interpretation takes the prefix in a negative sense, and paraphrases the word by 'the absence of becoming (*bhava*).' This view is apparently supported by sòme *Nikāya* passages (S.III, 57, It. no. 49), and by the *Dhamma saṅganī* 1314. But it may be derived from them ; and it is odd that the word should have been found nowhere else in that sense. it is quite possible that the original sense was the usual one. At *Dhammapada* 282 it seems to mean decline in wisdom.

16. *Nekkhamma*. Burnouf (Lotus, 334)derives this word from *nis+karma*; Oldenberg (Vinaya Texts, I) from

nis+kama, and Childers (sub voce) from *nis+kramya*. These three derivations would give the meaning respectively as having no *Karma*, being devoid of lust, and going forth from home. Daramitipola explains it here as menaing either the second or third. No doubt Oldenberg is right as to the derivation. But Daramitipola is also right if we take his note as exegetical, not philological. The fact is that the derivation had been, from very early times, forgotten or confused; and the connotation of the word was renunciation generally, with special reference to these two kinds. It never had anything to do with *karma*.

The three aspiratins of our paragraph here recur at *Saṃyutta* vol. II, 152, and on p. 151 *nekkhamma* is replaced by *kama*. See also Il. No. 72. and *Majjhima Nikāya* vol. I. p.- 114.

17. Aññā : *one of the many epithets of Arahantship.*

III
Ānāpāna Sati Sutta[1]

Translated By
Lord Chalmers.

Thus have I heard. Once the Lord was staying at Savatthi in the old Pleasaunce in the palace of Migāra's mother, with numbers of well - known Elders and disciples, - the reverend Sāriputta, Mahā-Moggallāna, Mahā Kassapa, Mahā-Kaccāyana, Mahā-Koṭṭita, Mahā-Kappina, Mahā-Cunda, Anuruddha, Revata and Ānanda, toghether with other well known Elders and disciples. At the time the Almsmen who were Elders were instructing and teaching the novices, - some taking ten, others twenty or thirty or forty ; and under this instruction and teaching the novices grew to higher and higher specific attainments.

On the Sabbath of the full-moon at the end of the rains the Lord was sitting in the open in the moonlight, with the Confraternity gathered around him, when , observing silence to reign among them all, he addressed the Almsmen in these words : - I find content in this vocation ; in it I find contentment of heart. Wherefore, Almsmen, strive ever more and more zealously to attain the yet unattained, to gain the yet ungained and to realize the yet unrealised. I look to be back here again in Sāvatthī by Komudi, the fullmoon day of the fourth month.

When it reached the ears of the Almsmen belonging to that country that the Lord was expected back in Sāvatthī at this date, they came into the city to see the Lord ; the Elders grew keener and keener in instructing and teaching each their novices, - ten, twenty, thirty or fourty of them as the case might be ; and under this instruction and teaching the novices grew to higher and higher speciifc attainments. On the Sabbath of Komudi, on the fifteenth, the full-moon day of the fourth month, the Lord was sitting in the open in the moonlight, with the Confraternity gathered around him, when observing silence to reign among them all, he addressed the Almsmen in these words : There is no talking, all talk is stilled in this assembly which is set (as it were) in a shining mere. Such is this Confraternity of Almsmen - or a company like this, that it is worthy of oblations, offerings, gifts and homage and is the richest field in which to sow the seed of merit. Such is this Confraternity and such this company that a little thing given to it hereby becomes great and a great thing becomes greater still. Such a Confraternity or Company as this would be hard to find in the whole world. To see such a Confraternity and company as this it is worth journeying many a league carrying the burden of provisions for the journey. Such is this Confraternity and such is this company. Within this Confraternity there are *Arahantas*, - Almsmen in whom the Cankers are dead, who have lived the highest life, whose task in done, who have cast off their burden, who have won thier weal, who have destroyed all bonds that bounds them to the ceaseless round of existence, who have found the Deliverance of utter Knowledge. Within this Confraternity are return thence to earth. Within this Confraternity are Almsmen who, by destroying the three bonds and also by minishing passion malice and delusion, have become Onee returners and, on their last return to this world, will make an end of Ill. Within this Confraternity there are Almsmen who, by destroying the three bonds, are launched on the stream of salvation, safe from any evil doom hereafter, assured of their future, destined to find Enlightenment - of the Noble Eightfold Path - of friendliness to all - of compassion for all - of rejoicing with all - of poised equanimity - of pondering on foulness - and on the perception of trasiency.

Within this Confraternity there are Almsmen who live in the practice of cultivating mindfulness, by breathing exercises. If cultivated and developed mindfulness by breathing is very fuitful and profitable; — it perfects the four bases of mindfulness, which, being perfected, perfect the seven factors of enlightenment, which being perfected, perfect in turn Deliverance by comprehension.

How, Almsmen, is mindfulness by breathing cultivated and developed so as to prove very fruitful and profitable? - Take the case of an Almsman who, in the forest or at the foot of a tree or in an abode of solitude, sits crosslegged with body erect, with minfulness as the objective he sets before himself. In mindfulness he takes in breath and in mindfulness he exhales it; he knows precisely what he is doing when he is inhaling or exhaling either a long breath or a short breath; he schools himself, as he draws his breath in and out, to be alive to his body as a whole - or to still bodily factors - or to experience contentment - or to experience well being; he schools himself, in drawing his breath in and out, to experience the heart's several factors - or to still them - or to experience the heart as a whole several factors- or to satisfy the heart - or to keep the heart stedfast - or to set the heart free. He schools himself, in drawing his breath in and out, to dwelll on the impermanence of things - or on passionlessness - or on the cessation of things - or on eschewing them. This is how mindfulness in breathing is cultivated and developed so as to prove very fruitful and profitable.

How is mindfulness by breathing cultivated and developed so as to perfect the four bases of mindfulness ? While he is engaged in inhaling or exhaling, with a precise knowledge of what he is doing either when inhaling or when exhaling either a long breath or a short breath, when schooling himself either to experiecne the body as a whole or to still the several bodily factors, all this time in his contemplation of the body as an aggregation, the Almsman dewells ardent, alive to all he is doing, and mindful, quit of all worldly wants and discontents. Among the corporeal elements (earth, water, fire, and *air*) I classify breath inhaled or exhaled. Therefore the Almsman who contemplates the body as an aggregation, dwells the while ardent, alive to what he is doing, and mindful quit of all wordly wants and discontent while he is engaged in schooling himself in his breathing to experience contentment or well-being, or to experience the hearts's several factors or to still them, all this time, in his contemplation of feelings as an aggregation, the Almsman dwells ardent, alive to all he is doing, and mindful, quit of all worldly wants, and discontent. Among feelings, I classify thorough attention to breath inhaled or exhaled. Therefore the Almsman who contemplates feeling as an aggregation, dwells the while ardent, alive to all he is doing, and mindful. While he is quit of all worldly wants and discontent. While he is engaged in schooling himeself, as he inhales or exhales, to experience the heart as a whole, or to satify the heart, or to keep the heart stedfast, or to set the heart free - all this time, in his contemplation of the heart as an aggregation,the Almsman dwells ardent, alive to all he is doing, and mindful, quit of all worldly wants and discontent ; the man of distracted mind, say I, cannot develop mindfulness in breathing. While he is engaged in schooling himself, as he inhales or exhales, to dwell either on the impermanecne of things or on eschewing them, all this time, in his contemplation of mental objects as an aggregation, the Almsman dwells ardent, alive to everythimg, mindful, quit of all wordly wants and discontent. Discerning by understanding the abandonment of all wants and discontent, he surveys this theme exhaustively. Therefore, in his contemplation of mental objects as an aggregation, the Almsman dwells ardent, alive to all he is doing, mindful, quit of all worldly wants and discontent - This is how mindfulness in breathing is cultivated and developed so as to perfect the four bases of mindfulness.

How are the four bases of mindfulness cultivated and developed so as to perfect the seven factors of enlightenment? - While, in his contemplation of the body as an aggregation, the Almsman dwells ardent, alive to all he is doing, mindful, quit of all wordly wants and discontent, all this time his mindfulness is growing fixed and undistracted, with the result meanwhile that the factor of enlightenment which consists of mindfulness is implanted, that the Almsman develops it, and that it moves on the perfect development. Living thus mindful, he examines and scrutinizes, and analyzes the mental object with his understanding; and as he is doing so, the analytical factor of enlightenment is meantime being implanted, is being developed by the Almsman, and is moving on to its perfect developement, with the concomitant result that imdomitable zeal is implanted, and that this further factor of enlightenment is implanted, is developed by the Almsman and moves on to its perfect development.

To the man with zeal implatned in him comes satisfaction without alloy, and concomitantly the factor of enlightenment which consists in satsifaction is implanted, is developed by the Almsman, and moves on to its perfect development. The man with his mind satisfied comes to enjoy tranquillity alike of body and of heart, and concomitantly the factor of tranquillity is implanted, is developed by the Almsman, and moves on to its perfect development. The man with tranquillity and well-being of body finds concentration of heart, and concomitantly the concentration factor of enlightenment is implanted, is developed by the Almsman, and moves on to its perfect development. He surveys exhaustively as his theme his heart thus stedfast, and concomitantly the factor of poised equanimity is implanted, is developed by the Almsman, and moves on to its perfect development.

(And as it is with his contemplation of the body, so it is with his contemplation of feelings - of the heart - and of mental objects each resulting in the perfect development of the several factors of enlightenment). This is how the four bases of mindfulness are cultivated and developed so as to perfect the seven factors of enlightenment.

How are the seven factors of enlightenment cultivated and developed so as to perfect Deliverance by comprehansion ? - Take an Almsman who develops in turn each of the aforesaid seven factors of enlightenment each dependent on aloofness passionlessness and stilling, each maturing by Renunciation. - This is how is seven factors of enlightenment are cultivated and developed so as to perfect Deliverance by comprehension.

Thus sopke the Lord. Glad at heart, those Almsmen rejoiced in what the Lord had said.

Reference

1. *Majjihma Nikāya* (Sutta No. 118) Vol. III, pp. 79-88

Lord Chalmers (Tr.) *Further Dialogues of the Buddha* (Translation of *Majjihma Nikāya*) Vol. II, pp. 199-204.

IV

Kāyagatā Sutta[1]

Translated by
Lord Chalmers

Thus have I heard. Once when the Lord was staying at Sāvatthī in Jeta's grove in Anāthapiṇḍika's pleasaunce, and a great number of Almsmen were sitting in company together in the hall after their meal on return from their alms-round, the following talk arose among them : - It is wonderful, sirs, it is marvellous, to what a pitch the Lord who knows and sees, the *Arahat* all-enlightened, has cultivated and developed that mindfulness of body which is called the mindfulness abundant in fruit and blessings ! Here the talk broke off; for, when at evening the Lord arose from his meditations, he came to the seat set for him in hall, and asked what subject had engaged them in their conclave and what talk had been broken off. They told him, adding that here the talk had broken off, as the Lord appeared.

How, Almsmen, is midnfulness of body cultivated and developed so as to abound in fruit and blessings ? - Take an Almsman who, in the forest or at the foot of a tree or in an abode of solitude, sits crosslegged with body erect, with mindfulness as the objective he sets before himeself. In mindfulness he takes in breath and in mindfulness he exhales it; he knows precisely what he is doing when he is inhaling or exhaling either a long breath or a short breath; he schools himself, as he draws hims breath in and out, to be alive to his body as a whole or to still bodily factors.

As he dwells thus unflagging, ardent, and purged of self, all worldly thoughts that idly come and go are abandoned, and with their abandonment his heart within grows stablished and planted fast, stettled and concentrated. - In this way, an Almsman develops mindfulness of body.

Walking or sitting or lying down, in every posture of his body, he knows precisely what he is doing. As he dwells thus unflagging ... mindfulenss of body.

Again, the Almsman is always mindful and purposeful whether in going forward or back, in looking before or behind, in drawing in or stretching out his limbs, in conduct of cloak bowl and robes, in eating and drinking , in chewing and tasting, in attending to the needs of nature, in walking or standing or silent. As he dwell thus unflagging ... mindfulness of body.

Again, the almsman reflects on this self same body, from the soles of the foot to the crown of the head, as a thing bounded by skin and full of various impurities. There is in this body, says he, hair of head or body, nails and teeth, skin and flesh, sinews bones and marrow, kidneys heart and liver, pleura, spleen, lungs, inwards and bowels, stomach and faeces, bile, phlegm, pus, blood, sweat, fat, tears, serum, saliva, mucus, synovial fluid and urine. Just as if there was a two mouthed sack full of various grains - such as rice and paddy, beans and vetches, sesame and husked rice - and a man with eyes to see were to reflect as he emptied the sack that here was rice, there was paddy, here were beans, there were vetches, here was sesame and there husked rice; in just the same way does the Almsman reflect on this self-same body, from the sole of the foot to the crown of the head, as a thing ... synovial fluid and urine. As he dwells thus unflagging ... mindfulness of body.

Again, the Almsman reflects on this self-same body, whatsoever its position and posture, from the point of view of its elements, as containing within it the four elements of earth, water, fire and air. Just as a competent butcher or his apprentice, when he has killed a cow, might sit at the cross-roads, with the carcase and cut up into joints, even so does the Almsman reflects on this self same body, wheatsoever its position or posture. From the point of view of its elements, as containing within it the four elements. As he dwells thus unflagging ... mindfulness of body.

Again, just as it the Almsman were actually looking on a festering corpse after one two or three day's exposure in a charnel-ground, even so does he sum up this self same body as having these properties and this nature and this future before it. As he dwells thus unflagging .. mindfulness of body.

Agan, just as if the Almsman were actually looking on a corpse exposed in the charnel ground and there being devoured by crows or falcons or vultures or dogs or jackals or divers worms, even so dies he sum up this self smae body....(etc. as in prev. para).

Again, just as if the Almsman were actually looking on a corpse exposed in the chrnel-gourd, showing as a chain of bones either still with flesh and blood and sinews to bind them together, or with only smears of the flesh and blood left with the bones and sinews, or with the flesh and blood entirely gone, or with sinews gone and only the bones left scattered around, here a band and there a foot, here a leg and there an arm, here the pelvis, there the spine and there the skull, even so does he sum up this self same body....(etc. as inantepenultimate para) .. of body.

Again, the Almsman, divested of lusts and of wrong dispositions, develops in succession the First, Second, Third and Fourth Ecstasies (as in Sutta No. 39 etc.) As he dwells thus unflagging, ardent, and purged of self, all worldly thoughts that idly come and go are abandoned, and with their abandonment his heart within grows stablished and planted fast, settled and concentrated - In this way too the Almsman develops mindfulness of body.

If any Almsman whatsoever cultivates and develops mindfulness of body, deep into his bosom sink all right dispositions into which knowledge enters, - even as streams which flow down to the sea sink into the bosom of the ocean which the mind's eye surve. If any Almsman does not cultivate and develop mindfulness of body, Māra gains access; Māra can enter into him, It is just as if a man flung a heavy stone into a mass of wet clay. Would it find access?

Yes, Sir.

Just in the same way, if an Almsman does not cultivate and develop mindfulness of body, Māra gains access; Māra can enter into him. It is just as if there were a dry and sapless stick and a man came along and took it for his kindling wood to light a fire with and make a blaze. If he did so, could he by rubbing it make his fire burn up?

Yes, sir.

In just the same way, if an Almsman does not cultivate and develop mindfulness of the body, Māra gains access; Māra can enter into him. It is just like an empty water-jar on its stand with nothing in it and a man coming up to it with a load of water. Could he shoot his load into it?

Yes, sir.

In just the same way, if an Almsman does not cultivate and develop mindufulness of body, Māra gains access; Māra can enter into him.

But if the Almsmna does cultivate and does develop minduflness of body, Māra cannot gain access or enter into him.

It is just like a man throwing a light ball of string against the solid timbers of the door-posts. Would it find access?

No, sir.

It is just the same with the Almsman who has cultivated and has developed mindfulness of body ; - Māra cannot gain access or enter inot him. It is as if there were a wet stick with the sap still in it, and a man came along and took it for his knidling wood to light a fire and make a blaze. If he did so, could he by rubbing it make his fire burn up ?

No, Sir.

It is just the same with the Almsman who has cultivated and has cultivated and has developed mindfulness of body;- Māra cannot gain access or enter into him. It is just like a filled water-pot on its stand, full of water to the brim so that a crow could drink out of it. If now a man came along with a load of water, could he shoot his load into it?

No, sir.

It is just the same with the Almsman who has cultivated and has developed mindfulness of body - Māra cannot gain access or enter into him.

If any Almsman whatsoever has cultivted and developed mindfulness of body, then, in each and every intellectually realizable mental object to which he applied his mind for its intellectual relization, in every case he comes to be an eye witness thereof face to face, if there be an exercise of mindfulness. It is just like a square pond in a level expanse of ground with embanked sides and so full of water to the brim that a crow could drink out of it. If now a strong man were to break the containing embankment on this side and that, would the water run away through the breaches.

Yes, sir.

Just in the same way, if any Almsman has cultivated and has developed mindfulness of body, then... exercise of mindfulness. It is just like a carriage with a pair of thorough-breds harnessed to it and with the goad lying ready to hand, on level ground at the cross roads, - into which there mounts a skilled driver, who knows how to manage horses; with his left hand he takes the reins, grasping the goad in his right, and away he dreives, up and down, where he likes. Just in the same way, if any Almsman has cultivated and has developed mindfulness of body, then ... exercise of mindfulness.

If, Almsmen, mindfulness of body be practised, cultivated, developed, assimilated, made a basis, kept advancing, accumulated and vigorously pursued, ten blessings may be anticipated and they are these :-

He masters likes and dislikes ; - dislikes do not master him ; he is always victor over them if when they have arisen.

He masters fear and dread; they do not master him ; he is always victor over them if and when they have arisen.

He endures cold and heat, hunger and thirst, gad flies, mosquitoes, scorching winds, contact with creeping things, abusive and hurtful language; his nature is to bear all bodily feelings that are painful, acute, sharp, severe, wretched, miserable, or deadly.

The Four Ecstasies with their vivid illumination, which here and now bring well-being into life, - these he induces at will, without trouble or difficulty.

He develops the divers psychic powers ; - from being one to become manifold, from being manifold to become one, to be visible and invisible, to pass at will through wall or fence or hill as if in air, to pass in and out of the solid earth as if it were water, to walk on the water unbroken surface as if it were the solid earth, seated in state to glide through the air like a bird on the wing, to touch and to handle the sun and moon in their power and might, and to extend the sovereignty of his body right up to the Brahmā world.

By the Ear Celestial that is pure and far surpasses the human ear, he hears sounds celestial and sounds human both far and near.

His heart knows the hearts of other creatures and of other men, knows them for what they are, - the heart where passion dwells as passionate, the passionless heart as passionless, the unkind heart as unkind, the kindly heart as kindly, the deluded heart as deluded the undeluded heart as undeluded, the concentrated heart as concentrated the unconcentrated heart as unconcentrated, the great heart as great and the little heart as little, the inferior heart as inferior and the superior heart as superior, the stedfast heart as stedfast and the unstedfast heart as unstedfast, the heart Delivered as Delivered, and the undelivered heart as undelivered.

He recalls his own divers existences in the past, - a single birth, then two - etc.- divers existences in the past in all their details and features.

With the Eye Celestial that is pure and far surpasses the human eye, he sees creatures in act to pass hence, in act to reappear elsewhere, - creatures either lowly or debonair, fair or foul to view, happy or unhappy; and he knows well that they fare according to their past deeds.

By the extinction of the Cankers, he develops and dwells in that Deliverance of heart and mind where Cankers are not, a Deliverance which, of and by himself, here and now, he has discerned and realized.

These are the ten blessing, Almsmen, that may be anticipated, if mindfulness of body be cultivated in the way I have stated.

Thus spoke the Lord. Glad at heart, those Almsmen rejoiced in what the Lord had said.

Reference

1. *Majjhima Nikāya* (Sutta No. 119) Vol. III, pp. 89-99. Lord Chalmers (Trs.) *Further Dialogues of the Buddha* (Translation of *Majjhima Nikāya*) Vol. II, pp. 205-211.

V

Vipassanā : A Psycho-Spiritual Analysis

Harcharan Singh Sobti

Diligently practising the technique of *Vipassanā Meditation one learns to see things as they really are*. It is a psycho-spiritual discipline available to both men and women endowed with masculine temperament conducive to practise this technique, successfully. I propose to examine this hypothesis, in this brief introductory paper, in the background of Early Buddhist tradition and which calls for to identify the basic structure of THE WAY OF THE BUDDHA.

Bisexuality is a gift of nature, inherently, present in all human beings, in the sense that it combines both the masculine and feminine characteristics irrespective of being a man or woman. This psychological truth was discovered in India, long ago, and found its expression in the myth of *ardhanārīśvara*. We find a beautiful episode in *Śiva-purāna*[1] that tells us about the *ardhanārīśvara* form of Śiva. Brahmā, it is stated, commissioned *Prajapati*, the male being, to initiate the process of creation, but of no avail. Later on, Brahmā contemplated upon Maheśvara and latter appeared in the composite form consisting of male and female corporeal organism. This union of male and female takes the form of masculinity and femininity, ingrained in human psyche. *Sakhi Sampradaya*, founded by Swami Haridass of Mathura, contemporary of Akbar the Great and Guru of Tānasena the Immortal Singer, advoctes the view that 'there is only one Male and all others are females', has its roots in this very composite human psyche. The (male) adherents of this *Sampradaya* dress themselves like women, identify themselves with Radha and conduct themselves, likewise. Those who are attracted towards this kind of devotion to Iśvara in the form of Krishna, certainly, imbibe disproportionate quanity of feminie traits in their psychic beings. It is a case of projecting femininity rooted in the male biological organism.

The fact of human beings imbibing composite psychic nature is also acknowledged by Gurū Nanak (1469-1539 A.D.) the Founder Gurū of Sikhism, when he categorically states that :

> "There is a woman in man and man in woman only the wise can discern it."[2]

Bisexuality as a psychic phenomenon is a subject of study in modern psychology, as well. " Every individal ....." discovered Sigmund Freud (1856-1939), " displays a mixture of the charactertraits belonging to his own and to the opposite sex ; and he shows a combination of activity and psssivity whether or not these last character-traits tally with his biological ones"[3] Freud indentified activity in woman as a masculine trait and passivity in man as feminine one. An activity and passivity, as such, one may aruge, has its roots in male dominant society. Anyhow, psychologically speaking every individual is to be viewed in this background.

The Buddha on the one hand was reluctant to admit women into *Saṅgha* and on the other he endorsed the query of Ānanda as regard to the capability of woman for realizing 'the fruit of conversion ....' when, 'entered the homeless state, under the doctrine and discipline proclaimed by the Blessed one.' "Woman is capable".[4] Here, woman is viewed as a psychological being that imbibes both the masculine and feminine character-traits. The capability of woman as a psychological being is directly linked with 'the doctrine and discipline proclaimed by the Blessed One'. What is there in woman and doctrine that goes well with each other ? The basic thing in the doctrine is that it is meditative in nature. In order to draw any benefit from the doctrine and discipline of the Buddha it is imperative that it suits the temperament of the person concerned.

In Early Buddhist tradition even an obeject of meditation needs to be selected with the guidance of *Kalyānamitta*, according to one's temperament.[5] So, it is a temperament of the person pursuing religious discipline that works as a deciding factor and any deviation from the path, therefore, is hardly helpful.

As stated earlier the Buddhist descipline is meditative (and not devotional) in its approach. Now whether it suits the masculine or feminine temperament, it is yet to be examined. Masculinity in its contents is through and through assertive, active and hence egoistic. It is difficult for a person having an overall masculine temperament to accept 'the other'. It is the prerogative of feminine temperament alone to accept 'the other' and melt oneself therein. There is 'no other' as is found in *sakhi-sampradaya,* in Early Buddhist tradition conducive as an object of devotion that feeds feminine-self. The WAY OF THE BUDDHA is satisfying only for those imbibing masculine temperament.

The Buddha's acceptance of 'Capability of woman' to become *arahata* after successfully practising *vapassanā* and consequent upon that actually seeing *anicca, anatta* and *dukkha* the three marks of phenomenal existence, refers to the masculinity inherent in her psychic being. And, this conclusion must be rejected if it fails to secure substantive support from the canonical text, namely, *Therīgātha*. Mrs. C.A.F. Rhys Davids in the Introduction to *Psalms of the Sisters* (translation of *Therīgtātha*), has made certain observation useful for our present discussion. While drawing a distinction between Indian Marys and their Christian sisters, she notes that :

> "But herein we note a sharp contrast between those Indian Marys and their Christian sisters. There He, the Central-figure, intervenes, and gratitude is blent with adoration, the little poem (*Therīgātha*) reveals

> no word of quasi amorous self surrender to the person or Image of the Beloved, such as characterizes not a little of that Christian literature for which the song of Solamon - 'I am my beloved's and my beloved is mine' - was a sacred archetype.[6]

Again, Mrs. Rhys Davids comments that:

> " The utmost a *theri* presumes to go in relating herself to her teachers is to claim spiritual fatherhood in Him."[7]

To add further Mrs. Rhys Davids holds the view " that of the four notorious Magdalens who found peace and purity in the Order of *Bhikkhunis* - Addhakasi, Vimla, Abhay's mother and Ambapali - not one expresses any deep feeling of personal attachment to the Teachers."[8] The possibilities of imbibing feminine traits such as, 'self-surrender' and 'deep feeling of personal áttachement' by the *theris* whose life sketches and verses certifying the fact of having attained *arahathood*, we find in *Therīgātha*, are ruled out. These *theris* are, therefore, exceptional women being dominantly masculine in their mental disposition. This is also borne by the fact that"life under the Vinaya was one of both active and contemplative discipline."[9]

So, masculinity at a psychic level and of a higher order is a prerequisite for entering into the realm of *vipassanā*. Here, we would like to point to one more distinction between *jhāna* and *vipassanā*. Rev. Henepola Guṇaratna in his recent book *The Path of Serenity aud Insight*[10]. has identified two kinds of disciples : (i) disciples of a contemplative bent and (ii) disciples of an intellectual bent. One with contemplative bent of mind prefers to conquer the *nīvaraṇa* or hindrences five in number viz. *kāmacchanda, vyāpadā, thina-middha, Uddhaccakukkucca* and *vicikicchā*, through *jhāna* gaining *samatha* (serenity) and thereafter moves on to the development of *vipassanā (insight). The diciples imbibed with intellectual bent* of mind follows a different course. He moves on straightway to develop *vipassanā* without undergoing a practice of *jhāna*. The first kind of Buddhist disciple i.e., *samathayānika* is stated to develop "insight preceded by serenity." The latter one with intellectual bent of mind follows direct course and develops "serenity preceded by Insight" and is therefore called *vipassanāyānika*.

Our main concern, at the moment, is *vipassanā* and which can be available to only those who imbibe masculine temperament combined with intellectual bent of mind. This insight into the basic structure of *the WAY OF THE BUDDHA also* amounts to *see things as they really are.*

References

1. J.L Shastri (Ed.) *Ancient Indian Tradition and Mythology : Śiva-purāṇa* (Satarudra Saṁhita) Chapter III, vol. II, Part II.

   cf., Gopi Nath T.A. *Rao, Elements of Hindu Iconography*, Vol .II, Part I. pp. 331-331.

2. Ādi Granth (Holy Book of the Sikhs). *Sri Damdami Biṛ, various printed editions. Standard Pagination 1430 pp. p. 879.*

3. James Strachey, (Gen. Ed.) *The Complete Psychological Works of Sigmund Freud.* Vol. VII. p. 220.

4. Rhys Davids, T.W. and Hermann Oldenberg, (Trs.) *Vinaya Texts* Part III. P. 322.

5. For detailed analysis see ;

   Bhikkhu, Nanamoli, *The Path of Purification* (Translation of *Visuddhimagga*). pp. 102 ff.

6. C.A.F. Rhys Davids *Psalms of the Early Buddhists : Psalms of the sisters - 1 (translation of Therigātha)* p. xxxii.

7. *Idem*

8. *Ibid.* p. xxxiii.

9. Ibid. p. xxxiv.

10. Henepola Gunaratana, *The Path of Serenity and Insight,* pp. 38-39.

VI
The Contemplation of Breathing
(Ānāpāna-sati)
Vimalo

There are quite a variety of approaches to the use of the breath as a vehicle of contemplation. Some people use the sensations of the breath at the nostrils as the meditation object, othęrs keep the attention on the rising and falling of the abdomen, some breathe heavily in order to have a clear meditation object, and others count each breath.

I find it interesting that the Buddha never mentioned where one should watch the movement of breathing. If one is sufficiently in touch with the breath, it might not be necessary to choose a specific place in the body where one contemplates the breath; rather one puts the attention where the movement of breathing is most clearly felt. The movement of the diaphragm creates a wave which passes, if there are no blockages, throughout the whole body, and that movement can be felt from the toes to the crown of the head.

Many people, as soon as they watch the breathing, cease to have a free flowing breath. They hold or control. it . To have a free flowing breath which is not controlled by the conscious mind is a great help for relizing the real depth and potential of the contemplation of breathing. The question is only : how can one learn to allow the breath to find it's own natural, unimpeded rhythm and yet be fully aware of it ?

It is important to learn not to interfere with the breath. Many people feel quite lost if they can't control or direct or manage things. In meditation we have to develop the opposite faculty more, namely pure sensitivity, allowing things to unfold by themselves without interference from the conscious mind.

In a Breathing Workshop with Ilse Middendorf, I came across a number of meditative exercises which enable one to gradually feel the movement of breathing throughout the whole body. With the help of these exercises one can also learn not to interfere with the natural flow of the breath. I have found these exercises so helpful that I now work with a breath therapist at meditation retreats who gives every day breathing exercises and also, if necessary, individual treatment. Each of these exercises 'opens' a particular part of the body so that slowly the whole body becomes more alive and the breath can flow freely throughout.

Since many people in the West have a fair number of inner blockages and are rather alienated from their bodies, they are often not in touch with their breathing. Being aware of the particular difficulties of most Western people which prevent them from going more deeply into meditation or drag them down soon after a meditation course, I feel it is something of the famous Buddhist 'skill of means' (*upāya-kauśalyatā*) if we integrate some of the bodily 'know-how' developed in the West, some of which has a direct bearing on the meditation. For example, the Alexander Technique can be a great help in learning to sit with less pain and at the same time becoming more aware of how we use our bodies in daily life. Being more in touch with the body and breath is a great help in carrying awareness over into daily life and becoming more aware of what one is doing. If we are not in touch with our bodies there is no joy in turning one's attention to the body, and so the mind turns to day-dreams, fantasies, and discursive thinking.

In Buddhism we have a somewhat one-sided emphasis on the mind, and consequently the need, especially with Western people, to integrate the body, is rather neglected. This is quite typical wherever there is a strong monastic tradition. In this age of ours it seems to me that we have to learn to use all the challenges of life as possible means for inner growth, and that means a more holistic approach, developing in a creative way 'skill of means' and applying the principles of the spiritual life in every-day life situations. 'Skill of means' is to know intuitively in any given situation what would be the most appropriate way of handling that challenge.

The different schools of *vipassanā* meditation teach different methods and approaches to the development of awareness. Some stress the needs for the mind to focus on a narrow field or object to the exclusion of everything else. Others teach the development of a more comprehensive awareness. It seems to me that awareness, as the Buddha originally taught it, includes on the one had the ability to focus on any particular object and on the other hand to be open and receptive to whatever presents itself at any of the six sense doors. Awareness, *satipaṭṭhāna*, has a greater depth and richness if one has developed the ability to focus the mind and also to stay in a state of comprehensive awareness.

People who have learnt to focus or concentrate on particular objects find comprehensive awareness at first rather difficult and become somewhat restless when they direct the awareness to the whole body. If they continue they often discover a new kind of 'spaciousness of consciousness'. One can develop this more spacious quality of awareness by slowly extending the field of attention.

Reading the *Ānāpānasati-sutta*, the text in the Pali Canon where the Buddha describes the different aspects of the contemplation of breathing, one is struck by the fact that the emphasis is on some sort of very comprehensive awareness. The Buddha says we should be aware of the breath and also of the whole hody, of the breath and of the feelings, of the breath and the state of mind, of the breath and the contemplation of impermanence, etc.

Being aware of the breath and also of the feelings means to notice the interrelationship of feelings and breathing. The same applies to the mind. Each state of mind changes the breathing in subtle ways, and vice versa. This might give rise to insights into the interdependence of all things, which is quite important in the Mahāyāna.

The Buddha also recommends being aware of the breathing and at the same time seeing from moment to moment all feelings, sensatons, and perceptions as impermanent. This is a genuine *vipassanā* contemplation and presupposes a considerable steadiness of the mind.

The Buddha said that there are two differnet aspects of meditation : *samatha*, inner stillness, and *vipassanā*, insight. I have the impression that he used these terms (and many others) somewhat differently than they are generally understood nowadays. When people today use these terms, they mean 'methods of meditation', but the Buddha used them more to describe states of consciousness. Another differnece is that the Buddha spoke very highy of *samatha* and of the Jhānas, while nowadays mainly *vipassanā* meditation is emphasised, and *samatha* and the *Jhānas* are often down-graded, and their true significance is not appreciated. My own experience is that the practice of awareness, *satipaṭṭhāna,* leads both to inner stillness (*samatha*) and to insights and clarity (*vipassanā*).

The Buddha said that if one has *samatha*, one should also develop *vipassanā* and if one has *vipassanā* but has not yet found inner stillness or peace of mind, one should develop that as well.

What significance does inner stillness have for the spiritual path ? I think one of the mot important values of a still mind is to be more centred and to find some higher form of happiness within oneself. If through meditation one finds serenity and peace of mind, then quite a few things become somewhat irrelevant. A profound inner stillness has also a liberating effect.

Inner stillness is, so to speak, the 'breeding gound' for countles positive states of mind which may arise spontaneously ; for example, the *jhānas* or the seven enlightenment factors. It is significant that the Buddha never says how one develops the *jhānas*. If the mind is still, then the joy and bliss which characterise the first two *jhānas* may arise and may later go over into the peace of the third *jhāna*.

At first most meditators find it very difficult to stop thinking. Even though trying to stay with the meditation obejct, they catch themselves again and again thinking, planning, remembering, living in the past or in the future. If the awareness becomes stronger, there may be just a single thought going through the mind before one becomes aware of it. If the awareness is further strengthened, one may become aware of thinking when a train of thought has just started, and the awareness is then like a sword cutting through it.

For a long time we have kept the mind busy, and many people believe that the main function of the mind is to think. Though it is very important to have the ability to think clearly, it is equally important to develop the opposite quality, namely to learn to stop discursive thinking. One comes to it by bringing the mind always back to the meditation and by learning to really surrender to the meditation and giving one's total attention to it. If one finds some serenity and inner stillness, it becomes easier because one sees how unsatisfactory the inner chatter really is. The more there is of real inner stillness, the more we realise that the true nature of our mind is pure awareness.

The Buddha said that there are two kinds of meditation: *sasankhārika* and *asankhārika samādhi*. *Sansankhārika samādhi* means that one is directing the attention. If one feels tiied or sleepy, one puts some more energy into the meditation ; if the mind is more steady, one directs it to a more comprehensive awareness or to perceiving from moment to moment that all phenomena are impermanent processes. But all this is still directing the mind. In those moments of real inner stillness when the mind is neither 'for' nor 'against' something, one may catch a glimpse of that effortless state of *asankhārika samādhi.* Hui-Hai, one of the great Chinese Zen masters, called this effortless state the 'non-abiding of the mind'.

The contemplation of breathing can be like an ever-present anchor for holding the awareness; it may help us to be more in touch with our bodies and with ourselves, and help us explore the depth and richness of meditation.

VII
Mindfulness on Breathing (Āṇāpānasati)
H.S. Shukla

Lord Buddha, in his *dhammic* way-faring, initiated his *Dhamma,* manifesting basically in two forms : as a psycho-ethical system of thought as well as a practical way of gradual purification. As a thought it presents a minute analysis of a man, the suffering associated with him, its causes and the possiblity of tis eradication. As a path it proceeds with right efforts for gradual purifiction and culminates in realization of a state of Supramundane bliss. These two streams always flow together like the two wheels of a chariot. One functions as the theory (*Pariyatti*) and the other as the practice (*Patipatti*). In the absence of any one of them, it remains incomplete and unbalanced. In the course of his way-faring, Lord Buddha, as a practical way, introduced an ideal of *Satipaṭṭhāna Bhāvanā* which is the only way, that leads to the purification of beings, to the passing beyond sorrow and lamentation, to the cessation of sufferings and miseries, to the attainment of the Noble path and to the realization of *Nilbāna* :

> *"Ekayāno ayaṁ, bhikkhave, maggo sattanaṁ visuddhiyā, sokaparidevānam samatikkamāya dukkhadomanssanaṁ aṭṭhaṅgamaya, ñāyassa adhīgamāya nibbanāssa sacchikiriyāya, yadidaṃ cattāro satipaṭṭhānā."* [1]

The word 'Satipaṭṭhāna' has two component parts : *Sati* and *upaṭṭhāna*. *Sati* means mindfulness or awareness and *upaṭṭhāna* stands for presence of application. Thus

Satipaṭṭhāna means application of mindfulness which is firmly established. It has the characteristic of remembering which means opposition to forgetfulness and the manifestation of watchfulness. [2]

The way of *Satipaṭṭhāna* consists of four parts . They are:

1. *Kayānupassanā Satipaṭṭhāna,*
2. *Vedanānupassanā-Satipaṭṭhāna,*
3. *Cittānupassanā-Satipaṭṭhāna,*
4. *Dhammānupassanā-Satipaṭṭhāna.*

They are firmly established on physical phenomena, sensation, thoughts or mental processes and the phenomena as *nīvraṇās* etc. respectively.

Of the four *Kayānupassanā Satipaṭṭhāna* is contemplation of the physical aggergate called body. There are fourteen ways of contemplating on the body. The first is *Ānāpānasati* or mindfulness on breathing. The second is fontemplation of walking, standing, sitting, and lying down (*Iriyapatha*). The third is about the comprehension on physical actions such as moving forward, moving backward etc. Which is called *Sampjana*. The fourth one is the consideration of repulsiveness (*patikula-manasikara*). It is the contemplation on the thirty-two parts of the body like hairs of the head, hairs of the body, nails, teeth, skin etc. The fifth is *Dhātumanasikara,* which means developing insight by contemplating four elements such as earth, water, fire and air. The remaining nine contemplations are comparing one's body with a dead body to arouse loathsomeness.[3]

The present paper is intended to offer a brief exposition of Mindfulness on Breathing (*Ānāpānasati*) as it appears in Early Buddhist texts.

Mindfulness on Breathing is an English rendering of the term '*Ānāpānasati*'. The word '*Ānāpānasti*' has three component parts such as *Āna* + *Apana* + *Sati*. *Āna* menas inhaled breath or inbreathing, *Apana* means exhaled breath or out breathing and *Sati* stands for minduflness or awareness. Thus, the word *Ānāpānasati* means mindfulness on in-breathing and out-breathing. It is one of the forty *Kammaṭṭhānas*. The word *Kammaṭṭhāna* is a technical term used for the object of meditation. Literally it means the place of action. But here the action is restricted in the sense of *jhānic* action. Therefore, the *Kammaṭṭhāna* is the name of place where *jhānic* action is performed. In this context it should also be known that all forty types of *Kammaṭṭhānas* are not suitable to all types of persons. They are given according to the temperatment of the person concerned.[4] The *Yogāvacara,* with the help of *Kalyānamitta*, selects one of them. In respect of *Ānāpānāsati*, it is stated that the reflection on breathingis is suitable to such persons who are of dull temperament (*Mohacarita*).[5]

After taking the object of meditation, he is adivsed to select a place for practice. First of all he should get an opportunity to live in the same monastery with his teacher and start his practice of meditation under his guidance and do his duties towards him. If not possible, he should select another monastery at a suitable distance. He should be particular in avoiding a place which is not suitable. According to the earlier texts the suitable places for the purpose are the secluded dwelling, a forest, the foot of a tree, a mountain, an open field and the heap of straw.[6] The *Visuddhimagga* also mentions five qualities of a suitable place. It should be neither too far from the village nor too near. It should be little frequented in the day and remain tranquil in the night. There should be no external disturbances such as from creeping creatures, serpents and so on. It should be inhabited by the learned monks.[7]

Further, the *Vishddhimagga* enumerates eighteen types of places which are regarded as unsuitable for the purpose. They are the large monastery, a monastery under construction, ruined or dalapidated monastery, a monastery situated along a highway or on the bank of a pond, a monastery in the city, a monastery situated on the border of the country and so on.[8]

After selecting a suitable place and object of meditation (*Kammaṭṭhāna*), the *Yogāvacara* makes efforts for developing concentration. It is evident from the text that mind is pure and luminous by its nature and defiled by incoming defiling forces.[9] Thus it loses its own natural form and it becomes fickle, restless and unsteady.[10] It wanders here and there and fosters attachment with various types of objects and indulges in sensual pleasure. The higher degree of attachment creates greater degree of suffering. Therefore, to bring it back to its natural form, he shold proceed for th parctice of meditation When he starts meditation, the causes of fickleness of mind called *Nīvaraṇa,* make it restless. They put obstacles and do not allow concentration on an object. They are the *Kāmachanda, Vāpāda, Thīnamiddha, Uddhaccakukucca* and *Vickcicchā.*[11] *Kāmacchanda* is the strong urge for sensual pleasure, *Vyāpāda* is ill-will or antipathy. *Thīnamiddha,* means sloth and torpor. Laziness connected with mental states is *thina* and laziness connected with consciousness is called *Middha. Uddhaccakukucca* stands for worry and flurry. It is bewildering of mind and brooding over what is done and what is not done. *Vicikiccaā* means doubt. In the technical sense, it is doubt in the *Buddha, Dhamma* and *Saṅgha.*[12]

In addition to these five hindrances, there are others too. They are called *Pālibodha*. They function also as impediments in creating attachment with various objects as well as in developing sluggishness in meditational efforts. They are place (*Āvāsa*), family (*Kulaṁ*), gain (*Lābho*), group of followers (*Gaṇa*), construction work (*Kammaṁ*), travel (*addhānaṁ*), relatives (*Nāti*), affection (*Ābādho*) book (*Gantha*) and supernatural power (*Iddhi*). So long as these are at work, it is very difficult to get concentration of mind.[13] So, they should get rid of before proceeding for meditation.

Now the *Yogāvacara* makes efforts for their suppression of hindrances etc. After due practice, the five hindrances along with others are suppressed. With their suppression, the constituents of *Jhāna* appear and help him in concentration of mind on the object.

How is the concentration on mindfulness of in-breathing and out-breathing developed ? In this context it is evident from the text that the *Yogāvacara* should go to a forest or the foot of a tree or a lonely palce and sit down with folded legs crosswised holding the body straight and upright. Then he should establish mindfulness in front of him.[14] Consciously he breathes in and breathes out. He is always mindful in breathing activites. He concentrates his mind in sixteen ways :

1. Breathing in for a long stretch he knows that he is doing so and breathing out for a long stretch he knows that he is breathing so.

2. While breathing in for short and breathing out for short, he knows that he is doing so respectively.

3. Experiencing its entry into the whole body he breathes in and feeling it goes through the whle body he breathes out. Thus he trains himself.

4. Calming down or tranquillizing the bodily aggregate or the activity of the body he breathes in and breathes out.

5. Feeling the thrill of zest or joy he breathes in and breathes out.

6. Experiencing rapture or the sense of ease he breathes in and breathes out.

7. Being aware of all mental factors or mind complex he breathes in and breathes out.

8. Tranquillizing the mental factors or mind complex he breathes in and breathes out.

9. He breathes in and breathes out experiencing the state of consciousness.

10. Gladdening the mind he breathes in the breathes out.

11. Concentrating the mind he breathes in and breathes out.

12. Releasing the consciousness free he breathes in and breathes out.

13. Contemplating impermancence he breathes in and breathes out.

14. Contemplating dispassion he breathes in and breathes out.

15. Contemplating cessation he breathes in and breathes out.

16. Contemplating[15] renunciation he breathes in and breathes out.

Now there is a question about the method of development of concentration on the object. In this contexdt it is stated that the *Yogāvacara,* after rightly following the *Sīla,* should take up meditation in five stages from the teacher. The five stages are : learning (*Uggaho*), questioning (*Paripuccpa*), establishing (*Upathanam*), application (*appana*) and characteristic (*Lakkhanam*).[16] Learning is the learning of the subject of meditation. Questioning is asking on the subject. Establishing is establishing the meditation subjefct. Application is the focussing of the subject. And chracteristic is the characterizing of the subject.[17]

There is a process of concentration on the mindfulness of in-breathing and out breathing. The process consists of eight stages. They are the : (1) Counting (*Ganana*), (2) Connection (*Anubandhana*), (3) Touching (*Pusana*), (4) Fixing (*Thapana*) (5) Noting or observing (*Sallakkhana*), (6) Turning away (*Vivatthana*) (7) Purification (*Parisuddhi*) and (8) Looking back of these (*Patipassana*). The text presents that '*ganna anubandhana puhsana thapana sallakkhana vivatthana parasuddhi tesam ca patipassana*.'[18]

Counting is just counting the number of breathings. The *Yogāvacara*, who is beginner, should attend to the subject first by means of counting. When he starts counting, he should not count as one, three, five or two, four, six and so on. Or he should stop counting and resume it after a little gap. Further it is also mentioned that in counting the meditator should reither stop short of five nor go beyond ten, nor should make any break in the series. When he stops short of five, the state of consciousness becomes restless and when he goes beyond ten, the state of consciousness is dependent on the number instead of the subject (breaths). When the series is broken, his mind trembles and wanders.

How should he start counting ? Keeping these faults in his mind and avoiding them, he should at first begin counting slowly as a grain measurer does. Taking the in-breath or the out-breath whichever appears, he should begin with one, and count upto ten, noting it as it arises each time. As he does his counting in this way, the in-breaths and out-breaths become evident to him. Now he can leave off slow counting and can count quickly one, two ... ten. Now the subject appears like a continuous series and then it proceeds without a break.

But here there is a question about the period. How long is he to go on counting ? Until without the help of counting his mindfulness is established on the breathings as object, because his counting serves the purpose of cutting off thoughts which run after external things. [19]

After giving up the counting, he should direct attention by means of connection. Connection is the ceaseless pursuit of breathings by mindfulness. In this context it has been stated that there are three steps of breathings. They are : beginning, middle and end. Of the outgoing breath navel is the beginning, the heart is the middle and the nose-tip is the end. Of the in-coming breath the nose-tip is the beginning, the heart is the middle and the navel is the end. Further it is advised that he should not concentrate his mind through these three steps because if it is done the mind and the body become distrubed, waver and tremble. Therefore, he should do so not by the beginning, middle and the end rather by touching and fixing.[20]

Actually, there is no attention to be given to it by touching separate from 'fixing. Indeed, in counting the breathings at the point of contact he gives attention to them by counting and touching. After giving up counting at the point of contact he is connecting them by means of mindfulness in the same place and fixing consiousness by absorption. Then he attends them by means of connection, touching and fixing. The great commentator, Buddhaghosa has made it very clear by giving simile of a gate-keeper. Just as the gatekeeper does not examine the people within and without the town by asking some question. But he examines each and everyone who comes to the door. So the *Yogāvacara* is not concerned with the in-coming and out-going breaths but only with the breath that reaches the door (nostril). He is not unaware of these three things. Therefore the text makes it clear that :

> *Nimittaṁ assasapassasa anarammanamekacittassa,*
>
> *Ajanato ca tayo dhamme bhavana nupalabbhati.*
>
> *Nimittaṁ assasapassasa anarammanakemacittassa,*
>
> *Janato co tayo dhamme bhāvanā upalabbhatiti.*[21]

The sign, in breath and out-breath are not the the object of the single consciousness. But one who does not know these three things, can not attend developmenmt and one who does know these three things, can attend dvelopmenmt on the subject. Thus it is apparent that keeping the knowledge of these three things, the *Yogāvacara* should attain concentration. Firstly he should mark the original point of contact of breathings. The in-breaths and out-breaths occur striking the tip of the nose or the upper lip of the mouth. Thus he should fix the sign on the place of striking. He should not look anywhere for the purpose than the original points of contact. Otherwise no concentration on breathings can be attained. Because of this condition, Lord Buddha is not seen in favour of development of the mindfulness on breathings for one who is forgetful and unknowing.[22]

After marking the sign on the point of contact he should repeatedly apply himself to the object of meditation. Applying so the image appears like a star, a ball of ruby or a ball of pearl, to some a soft touch like silk-cotton or a breeze etc. to some it has a harsh touch like a cotton-seed etc. and so on. It is due to the differences in perception, and one subject of meditation appears differently because it is born of perception. After this he should fix the mind on the images. Doing so his hindrances are suppressed and defilements subsided. With the suppression of hindrances mindfulness is set up and the mind is well fixed with concentration.

Further he should not attain the image for its colour and characteristic but he should only guard the image as carefully as the kings's chief queen guards her child in her womb, and makes it grow and improve with repeated attention. In course of such practice, the Fourth and Fifth *Jhānas* are achieved by him on the same image. Now *Yogāvacara* wants to reach purity by developing the subject through noting. So he should practice the *Jhānas* by means of adverting, entering upon, making up the mind, emerging and by reflection until he determines mind and matter insight.

How is it possible ? It is possible through insight knowledge. In his due practice he sees that the in-breathes and out-breathes have the physical body and the mind as their origin. So on account of the body and mind the breath is set in motion. Now he defines the breathings and the body as matter and mind and mental state assiciated with it as 'immaterial'. Having defined thus he searches for their cause. He puts porward the three characteristics (*Lakkhanam*) by contemplating aggregates in group and he puts away the ten imperfections like illumination etc. Further, he defines path and becomes detached and released from all conditioned things. After that he becomes an *Arahata* whose appetites are stilled, who is not absorbed in enjoyment, who has perceived void and unconditioned freedom (*Nibbāna*).[23]

References

1. *Dīghanikāya* Vol. II, p. 217 (Nalanda).
2. Bhikkhu Nyaṇmoli, *The Path of Purification*, p. 187.
3. *Dīgha Nikāya* Vol. II, pp. 217-221
4. Dwarka Das Shastri (Ed, *Visuddhimagga* p.88.
5. *Ibid*
6. *Majjhima Nikāya* Vol.I p. 61 (Nalanda). *Saṃyutta Nikāya* Vol. V p. 265 (Nalanda).
7. Dwarka Das Shastri op.cit. p. 95.
8. *Ibid* pp. 95-98
9. *Aṅguttara Nikāya* Vol.I p. 10 (Nalanda)
10. *Khuddaka Nikāya* Vol.1 p. 20 (Nalanda)
11. *Dhammasgaṅgani* pp. 258-259 (Nalanda)
12. *Idem.*
13. Dwarka Das Shastri op. cit. p.72
14. *Dīgha Nikāya* Vol.II p. 217 *(Nalanda) Samyutta Nikāya* Vol II. p. 265 (Nalanda)
15. *Saṃyutta Nikāya* Vol V. pp.265-266 (Nalanda)
16. Dwarka Das Shastri op. cit. p. 227
17. *Ibid* pp. 227-228.
18. *Ibid* p. 228
19. yava vina gananaya assasapassasarammane sati san-

tithati. Bahi visatavitakkavicchedam Katva assassapassasarammane satisanthapanattham yeva hi gannana ti. Dwarka Das Shastri op. cit. pp. 220-221.

20. *Ibid*, p. 321.

21 *Khuddaka Nikāya* Vol V. p. 199 (Nalanda)

22. Nahaṁ, bhikkave, mutthasatissa asampajanassa Ana pānassati-samadhi bhevanam vadāmi. *Saṁyutta Nikāya* vol. V p. 287

23. *Dhammapada Gātha*, 93.

VIII

Vedanānupassanā

Mahesh Tiwary

1. The preaching of the *Satipaṭṭhāna* is a unique in the history of Dhammic way -faring of the Buddha . Here and in this context alone, the Buddha appears as more than a perfect human being and with commanding emphasis initiates the path and explains its all-embracing fruit in the sublime words like--Here is "the one an only path, O Monks, leading to the purification of beings...to the realization of *Nibbāna*"[1] . In other places, he stands only as a guide and the activities are to be done by the persons concerned - *'Tumhehi kiccaṁṁ ātappaṁ akkhātaro tathāgatā*" . Here he prescribes the path, inspires one to set in on it properly, and himself stands as an ever alert witness to the latters's attainment of the either of the two stages of Sainthood- "*Diṭṭevadhamme aññā; sati vā upadisese anāgamita ti*"[2]

2. The worrd *Satipaṭṭhana* is interpreted in many ways. *Sat* means mindfulness. *Paṭṭhāna* denotes the sense of presence- "*Satìyā paṭṭhānaṁ* expresses the sense of arousing, making alert and functioning etc. In the light, making the mindfulness at work is the *Satipaṭṭhāna* — "*Saraṇaṭṭhena Sati, upaṭṭhānaṭṭhena paṭṭānaṁ. Iti sati ca sa paṭṭānaṁ cāti satipaṭṭhānaṁ pavattayitabbato ti attho.*" Again the term *Paṭṭhāna* means a sound base for making right efforts for gradually removing the layers of pollutions and realization of a state of Eternal Bliss-"*Padhānaṁ ṭhānam ti paṭṭānaṁ, satiyā paṭṭhānaṁ.*" In the sense, *Satipaṭṭāna* is the light of awareness which serves as a base for moral efforts for purificational gain[3].

The *Milinda-pañha* presents two more definitions of the term *sati.* Firstly, it is described as possessing the characteristics of reminding , making conscious of one's being a man (*manussa*), a rare creation, potential enough for acheiving higher spiritual gain as-"*apilāpaṇa-lakkṇanā sati*" . Secondly, it makes one aware of his moral and spiritual treasure for which he is generally not conscious of. The moral states like four-fold right efforts, (*vāyāma*), sevesn types of factors of enlightenment (*bojjhaṅga*), the twenty two types of sense-faculties (*Indriya*), the fives types of powers (*bala*) are the various gems of this treasure. It unearths them, makes them shining and arouses the real urge to have their conscious possession *-upagahana-Lakkhaṇā cā* it.'It is just like reminding and making aware of his possessions of a king by his chief minister.[4]

Sati is also treated as a doorkeeper-*dovāriko viya sati.* As the door-keeper when remains alert at the door, the undesirable persons do not dare to enter into the house; similarly on the presence of Mindfulness, the immoral states do not exert to harbour on the active surface of mind. Either they go deep down and remain dormant or become weak and functionless or are destroyed for ever.

All these shades of meaning, when analysed minutely, go to suggest that *Sati*, intrinsically is a ever-flowing stream of awareness possessed by a man as a natural gift. To tame the force of this stream, divert it the domain of moral states and keep it flowing in the same direction incessantly, is the *satipaṭṭhāna*. In this sense, it is briefly described as the Presence of Awareness.

3. *Satipaṭṭhāna* is fourfold as-*Kāyānupnssanā*, Vedanānupassanā, Cittānupassanā and *Dhammānupassanā*[5]. It has been stated as four, not more or less with full consideration of the benefits of the men to be led towards the state of *Nibbāna*. It is not advisable for all to follow all the four. Rather each one is beneficial for a group of people having similar type of psychic base. The flrst two viz. , the *Kāyānupassanā* and *Vedanānupssanā* are the paths for the persons with dominence of atachment (*Taṇhā-carita*)

and engaged in getting purification through the *Samatha*. There also the person exerting sluggishly in his process, takes *Kāyānupassanā* as his path and that who exert sharply chooses *Vedanānupassanā*. The consciousness of the former is gross in comparison to the latter. Further, the *Cittānupassanā* and *Dhammānupassanā* are the paths of the persons who are desirous of getting purification through *Vipassanā*. They are the persons of the temperament dominated by false view (*diṭṭhicarita*). One who is sluggish in his efforts, takes up *Cittānupassanā* as his path, whereas the man of sharp efforts follows the path of *Dhammānupassanā*. Here also, the consciousness of the former is gross in comparison to the latter. The commentator Buddhaghosa remarks in the conclusion that:

(a) *Samathayānikassa-mandassa akicchena adhigandhabbanimittaṁ paṭṭhamaṁ satipaṭṭhānaṁ visuddhimaggo,*

(b) *Tikkhassa olārikārammaṇe asanṭhahanato dutiyaṁ,*

(c) *Vipassanā-yānikassa mandassa nātippabhedagat-ārammaṇaṁ tatiyaṁ,*

(d) *Tikkhassa atippabhedagatārammaṇaṁ catutthaṁ.*[6]

From this it is evident that each of the four *Satipaṭṭhānas* is a complete path in itself. A man either knowing his temperament by himself or with the help of a *Kalyāna-mitta*, selects a path of his practice and thereby gets gradual purification and realization of the truths. Each one is regarded as a difinite path, potential to help in realizing the goal. It is the happy combination of both the *Magga* and *Ayana*, the path moving gradually towards the direction of minimisation of the layers of pollutions and in culmination of realization of *Nibbāna*. It is for this reason the two synonyms the *Magga* and *Ayana* have been used by the Master in his first Lion-roar-expression-"*Ekāyano ayaṁ, Bhikkhave, maggo Sattānaṁvisuddhiyā.... Nibbānassa sacchikiriyāya.*"

4. In the present background, here there shall be an humble attempt to present a brief description of only one path, the *Vedanānupassanā*. In doing so the meaning, the way of practice and fruits gained thereby will be taken into consideration.

5. The word *Vedanā* is derived from the root *vid* which means to experience. When an object comes in the range of a sense-organ, there is a simple contact of the same with mind through the medium of that sense-organ. Immediately after that, there follows the second reaction of mind to experience the object. It is called *Vedanā*. The nearest English word appears to be the feeling. Such reaction towards the object may be pleasant, painful or indifferent. Accordingly, there are three types of feelings. When the object is taken as agreeable, it is called pleasant feeling (*Sukhāvedanā*). On its being taken as disagreeable, it is called unpleasant feeling (*Dukkhāvedanā*). When it is taken as neither agreeable nor disagreeable, it is called indifferent feeling (*Upekkhāvedanā*). Further, the pleasant feeling may be physical and mental. The former is called *Sukhāvedanā* and the latter as *Somanassavedanā*. The unpleasent feeling is also of two types; physical and mental. The former is the *Dukkhāvednā* and the latter receives its expression as *Domanassa Vedanā* The indifferent feeling (*Upekkhā Vedanā*) is only mental. (The Suttantika tradittion maintains indifferent feeling also as physical and mental). In this way, there are five types of basic forms of feeling. The *Bahu-vedaniya-sutta* makes further analysis of feeling and puts it in as many as in hundred and eight varieties.[7] A whole chapter as many as thirty one discourses on *Vedanā* is available as *Vedanā-Saṁyutta-Nikāya*.[8]

Anupassanā has two componet parts-*anu* and *passanā*. *Anu* means seeing, observing etc. It literally means seeing consciously. continuously and minutely. Its psychological sense is to observe as it arises. The technical meaning of the term may be becoming continuously aware, and observing indifferently, without developing any string of attachment or of antipathy.

Thus *Vedanānupassanā* means becoming aware of the presence of the object it continuously and minutely, remaining completely detached from internal impact as their being agreeable, disagreeable or otherwise. It may be seen as under-

> Yathā pi vātā ākāse, vāyanti vividhā puthū,
> Puratthimā pacchimā cāpi, uttarā atha dakkhiṇā
> Sarajā arajā cāpi sitā uṇhā ca ekadā
> Ādhsmittā parittā ca, puthū vāyanti mālutā
> Atherimasmiṃ kāyasmiṁ samuppajjanti vedaıā
> Sukha-dukkha-samuppatti, adukkhamsukhā ca yā
> Yato ca bhikkhu ātāpī sampajaññaṃ na riñcaṭt,
> Tata so vedanā sabbā parijānātı paṇḍito.[9]

6. What for there is the practice of *Vedanānupassanā*? The plain and definite answer is for removal of suffering. This suffering is caused by attachment. The greater is the number of attacmhment, the bigger is the amount of suffering. The lesser number of attachment is the minimisation of the amout of suffering. The total reduction of the number of attachment leads to the total negation of suffering. This psychological state of desirelessness is the attainment of *Nibbāna*, a state of eternal bliss. It is for the attainment of this state, there is the practice of *Vedanānupassanā*. The following verse bears an evidence to the fact-

"So vedanā pariññāya, diṭṭhe dhamme anāsavo,

Kāyassa bhedā dhammaṭṭho saṅkhayaṃ nopeti vedagū"ti[10]

7. How it is practised ? A man, desirous of practising *Vedanānupassanā*, selects a place, sits in a seat cross legged, making body erect and keeping Mindfulness awakened around his face. He is at that time quite ardent, conscious and mindful with total destruction of greed and hatred towards the beings of the universe and prepares a soothing mental atmosphere for complete awareness of his own being, within and without. It is natural that in the background of

the contact, both internal and external, feelings arise. He on that occasion remains conscious and detached onlooker towards them. What-ever type of feeling may arise, he is aware of that, "The man, when affected by a feeling of pleasure, remains aware of it, reflecting- "I feel a pleasant feeling'. So, too, he is aware of the fact when affected by a painful feeling or by a neutral feeling." He perfectly knows that he feels an unpleasant or the neutral feeling on that occasion. In case of a pleasant feeling concerning material things, he remains conscious of that as "when affected by a feeling of pleasure concerning material things, remains aware of it, reflecting- "I feel a pleasant feeling concerning material things" . "When affected by pleasant feeling concerning spiritual things, remains aware and reffects- "I feel a pleasant feeling concerning spiritual thing. On arising of internal feeling he remains aware, and reflects-: I feel external feeling." There may be the occasion of arising of internal and external feelings simultaneously. In the situation he develops the same mental attitude tawards them. He remains aware and reflects- "I feel internal and external feelings". The process of his such detached awareness continues in every moment and the mind gradually becomes free from the thickets of attachment. During the course of continous paractice the mind becomes more and more subtle. With such a subtle mind, he starts reflecting over the arising of feelings together. "He keeps on consciously observing how the feeling as the *Dhamma* that comes to be" or the feeling as the *Dhamma* that passes away or the feeling as *Dhamma* both arises and passes away." He consciously remains aware and mindful that "there is feeling mindfulness etc. he obnserves with complete awareneess and self -collectedness. And so he abides completely detached, grasping after nothing in the world whatsoevesr." It means that in the process of practice there comes a moment when he reaches a state of complete detachment.[11]

8. In this context the words like '*ajjhata*' (internal) and "*bahiddha*" (external) deserve consideration. Buddhaghosa explains the word '*ajjhatat*' as concerning his own feeling

and *bahiddha* as the feeling of others. His expressions like--"*Iti ajjhattaṁ vā ti attano vā vedanāsu vedanānupassi, parassa vā vedanāsu; kālena vā attano, kālena vā parassa vedanasu vedanāupassi viharati*".[12] This interpretation, that he sometimes remains aware of his own feelings and sometimes of others, does not hold good in this context. A man sitting in a lonely place and practicing mindfulness with respect to 'Feeling,' remains completely in one place and in one process of thought. How can he develop practice with respect of other feelings sitting there? In the frame-work of this psychological situation such interpretation does not seem proper. In my view it appears logical to say that both the terms internal and external are connected with his own being. The waves of the feelings may pass internally through the psychic body of consciousness and psychic factors and also through his material body of consciousness and psychic factors and also through his material body generated by the four basic material qualities and twenty four generated material qualities. In course of remaining aware - of the arising etc., of feeling in his psychic body, he remains aware of the arising of internal feeling. And becoming aware of the arising etc., of feeling passing through his material body, he remains aware of the arising etc. of external feeling. In this way the interpretation of the terms *ajjhatta* and *bahiddha* appear to be more meaningful.

9. What may be the fruits of such practice ? It should be marked that the "Buddha's *Dhamma* has only one problem one definite goal and a path existing between the two. The one problem is the suffering which is caused by attachment. The definite goal is the attainment of *Nibbāna*. The path, in this context, is the practice of minfulness with respect to feeling. The path may be the Dhammic way-faring of any type. It takes one towards the state of eternal bliss by gradual minimisation of attachment. It may be marked that this practice of Mindfulness in respect of feeling consumates in complete detachment-*anissito ca viharati, no ca kinci loke upādiyati*". This state of desirelessness is the state of *Nibbāna* where survives alone the eternal bliss. In case, *Nibbāna* is not acheived either of the two fruits will

be the must. The Buddha, as a practical teacher, very clearly made the lion-roar- "In him one of the two kinds of fruition may be looked for;-either in this present life 'knowledge', or, if there be yet residual for rebirth,the state of him who returns no more."[13] Here the term knowledge refers to the state of *Sotāpanna* and the expression "who returns no more" to that of *Anāgāmi*.

References

1. *Digha Nikāya* Vol. II, p. 17 (Nalanda)
2. *Khuddaka Nikāya* Vol. I p. 42 (Nalanda)
3. *Sumaṅgalavilāsini* Vol III pp. 63-66
4. *Milinda Pañha pp. 39-40*
5. *DhammaSaṅgani* p. 100 (Nalanda)
6. *Sumaṅgalavilāsini* Vol III p. 66
7. *Majjhima Nikāya* Vol. II pp. 72-74 (Nalanda)
8. *Saṃyutta Nikāya* Vol. IV pp. 183-209 (Nalanda)
9. *Ibid* p. 194
10. *Ibid* p. 192
11. *Dīgha Nikāya* Vol. II, pp. 221-222 (Nalanda)
12. *Sumaṅgalavilāsini* Vol. III p.89
13. *Dīgha Nikāya* vol. II p. 235 (Nalanda).

IX
Samatha and Vipassanā - A Bird's - Eye View

Nathmal Tatia

1. The Nature and Function of *Samatha* and *Vipassanā*

The function of *Samatha and Vipassanā* are clearly explained in the following passages of the *Aṅguttara Nikāya*:

Monks, these two conditins lead to knowledge. What two ? *Samatha* and *Vipassanā* (tranquillity and introspection). If cultivated, what benefit does *Samatha* confer ? The mind is cultivated. What benefit does result from a cultivated mind ? All lust is abandoned (*yo rāgo so pahīyati*). Monks, if *Vipassanā* is to be cultivated, what benefit does it confer? Insight (*paññā*) is cultivated. If insight be cultivated, what benefit does it confer ? All ignorance is abandoned (*yā avijjā sā pahīyati*). A mind defiled by lust, monks, is not set free; not can insight defiled by ingorance be cultivated. Indeed, monks, the freedom from lust leads to release of the tranquillity of mind (*rāgavirāgā ceto-vimutti*), the freedom from ignorance leads to the release of the insight (*avijjāvirāgā paññā-vimutti*).[1]

Samatha and *Vipassanā* are compared to the pair of swift messengers (*Sīghaṃ dūtayugaṃ*), who carry the message of truth, that is, *Nibbāna* to the consciousness who is the Lord of the town, viz., the body, mindfulness (*sati*) being the gatekeeper of the six senses, and the Noble Eightfold Path being the way leading to *Nibbāna.*[2]

The purpose of *samatha* is to induce conentration in the mind and free it from all distraction (*Vikkhepa*). The essence of *Vipassanā* is to see the truth as it is (*anupassanā*). The two jointly act as a single harmonious entity as the way to *Nibbāna*.[3]

Sometimes an aspirant develops *Vipassanā* preceded by *Samatha* (*Samatha pubbaṅamam*). In him the fetters (*samyojanāni*) are abandoned, the lurking tendencies (*anusayā*) come to an end. Sometimes the aspirant develops *samatha* preceded by *Vipassanā* (*Vipassanā-pubbaṅgamamṃ)*. In him also, the fetters are abandoned and the lurking tendencies come to an end. Sometimes the aspirant develops *samatha* and *Vipassanā* together *(yuganaddhaṃ)*. As he does so, the fetters are abandoned and the lurking tendencies come to an end.[4]

We have mentioned that the essence of *Vipassanā* is *anupassanā*, that is, to see the truth as it is. Such *anupassanā* is practised by the discipline called *satipaṭṭhāna* which is translated as Foundations of Mindfulness (Retention of Mindfulness).[5] The discourses on *Satipaṭṭāna* occur at several places in the Pāli scriptures, for instance, in the twenty-second discourse of the *Dīgha Nikāya*, the tenth discourse of the *Majjhima Nkāya*, the forty seventh discourse of the *Saṃyutta Nikāya*, and the seventh *vagga* of the ninth *Nipāta* of the *Aṅguttara Nikāya*. The *Paṭisambhidāmagga* is also replete with passages that throw abundant light on the theme of *Satipaṭṭhāna*.

Exhorting his disciples to practise *Satipaṭṭhāna* in all earnestness, the Buddha said :

The one and only path, *Bhikkhus,* leading to the purification of beings, for overcoming sorrow and lamentation, for destroying pain and grief, for reaching the right path, for the realization of *Nibbāna* is the way of the fourfold Foundations of Mindfulness. These fourfold foundations are: (i) Contemplation of the Body, (ii) Contemplation of Feeling (iii) Contemplation of Mind, (iv) Contemplation of Mind-objects. These are practised by the aspirant, remaining ardent, self possessed and mindful, having overcome both the hankering and the dejection common in the world.

Ekāyano ayaṁ, bhikkhave, maggo sattānaṃ visuddhiyā, sokapaidevānaṃ, samatikkamāya, dukkhadomanassānaṃ atthaṃgamāya, ñāyassa adhigamāya, nibbānassa sacchikiriyāya - yadidam cattāro satipaṭṭhāna. katame cattāro? idha, bhikkhave, bhikkhu kāya kāyānupssī viharati ātāpī sampajāno satimā, vineyya loke abhijjhādomanassaṃ. vedanāsu vedanāupassi viharati ātāpī sampajāno satimā, vineyya loke abhijjhadomanassaṃ. citte cittānupassī viharati ātāpī sampajāno satimā, vineyya loke abhijjhadomanassaṃ dhammesu dhammānupassi viharati ātāpī sampajāno satimā vineyya loke abhijjhādomanassaṃ.[6]

II. *Satipaṭṭhāna* and *Ānāpāna*

Satipatthāha is the way to *vipassanā*, even as *Ānāpānasati*, is the way to *Samatha*. It is said that the meditator can put away the five hindrances (*nīvaraṇas*), the five sensual desires (*kāmaguṇas*), the craving for the five aggretates (*skandhas*), the five lower fetters (*orambhāgiyāni saṃyojanāni*), and the five upper fetters (*ouddhambhāgiyāni saṃyojanāni*) by practising the *Satipaṭṭāna*.[7] Of the four contemplation, the contemplation of the body consists of (i) mindfulness of breathing (*ānāpāna*), (ii) the postures of the body (*iriyāpatha*), (iii) mindfulness with clear comprehension (*samapajāna*), (iv) the reflection on the repulsiveness of the body (*paṭikūla-manasikāra*), (v) the reflection on the material elements (*dhātumanasikāa*) and (vi) the nine cemetery (*sīvathikā*) contemplations. In the contemplation of feelings, the meditator takes care that he does not cling to any sort of feelings, whether pleasant or painful or neutral. In the contemplation of mind the meditator perceives his mind as it is. He perceives the mind 'with lust' as 'with lust', 'without lust', as 'without lust,' 'with hate' as 'with hate', 'without hate- as 'wthout hate', and so on. In the contemplation of mind-objects, the meditator muses upon (i) the five hindrances, (ii) the five aggregates of clinging, (iii) the six internal and the six external sense-bases, (iv) the seven factors of enlightenment, and the four noble truths.

The close relationship between *Satipaṭṭhāna* and *Ānāpānasati* is brought out in the following passage of the *Majjhima Nikāya* :

> The *Ānapānasati*, mindfulness of in-breathing and out-breathing, monks, if developed and constantly practised, is of great fruit, of great advantage. Mindfulness of in-breathing and out-breathing, monks, if developed and constantly practised, brings to fulfilment the four foundations of mindfulness, *cattāro satipaṭṭhānā*. The four foundations of mindfulness, if developed and constantly practised, bring to fulfilment the seven links of enlightenment, *satta bojjaṅgā*, The seven links of enlightenment, if developed and constantly practised, bring to fulfilment freedom through knowledge, *vijjā-vimuttiṁ paripūrenti*.[8]

III. *Vipassanā* and the Threefold Nature of Things

By the practice of *Vipassanā*, the meditator gets an insight into the threefold nature of things, viz. impermanence, painfulness and substancelessness *aniccatā, dukkhatā* and *anattatā*. The most important impact of *Vipassanā* on the meditator's mind is his perception of constant change that is taking place in his body and mind. This leads to a proper understandings of the fact of *aniccatā*, impermanence of things, mental and material. From this experience of universal flux, the direct perception of the facts of *dukkhatā*, and *anattatā*, impersonaility or substancelessness of things, emerge in due course. Coming face to face with change, the meditator now starts to see things as they actually are, and feel that the frequency of change in an infinitesimal fraction of time is beyond his ken. The incessant change now challenges the meditator most vehemently to appreciate the fact of suffering. Gradually, the meditator arrives at the profound truth that all existence is devoid of an abiding substance of any sort. *Vipassanā* supplies novel information about one's emotions and passions and the working of one's mind, one's latent instincts and motives, and ultimately purges the mind of its defilements and evil tendencies. It also teaches to live with full awareness here and now and to look well before engaging in any act and take a complete view of things with circumspection and composure.

The right understanding of the nature of the pleasurable, painful and neutral feelings by means of *Satipaṭṭhāna* is the right way to the attainment of *Nibbāna*. This is indicated in the following passage of the *Saṃyutta Nikāya* :

Who sees the pleasure as pain,
And pain as a piercing barb;
Who sees as impermanent,
The state of feeling neutral;
That monk sees rightly indeed,
And feelings understands.
Understanding the feelings,
In this life is freed from intoxicants.
On the cessation of body, perfect in *dhamma*,
Crosses the world, past all reckoning.

Yo sukhaṃ dukkhato adda
dukkhamaddakkhi sallato/
Adukkhamsukkhaṃ santaṃ
addakkhi naṃ aniccato//
Sa ve sammaddaso bhikkhu
parijānāti vedanā/
So vedanā pariññāya
diṭṭhe dhamme anāsavo//
Kāyassa bhedā dhammaṭṭho
saṃkhyaṃ nopeti vedagū/[9]

IV. The Rationalism of The Buddha :

The thoroughgoing rationalism of the Buddha is reflected in many of his sermons. In one of his sermons, in connection with the practice of *Vipassanā,* he unreservedly asserts that one can realize the summum bonum of emancipation even in the absence of his loyalty to any faith or religious inclination or acceptance of any hearsay, or specious reasoning or delight in dogmas, simply by means of seeing things as they are. For instance, if the meditator has seen a form (or colour), or heard a sound, or smelt an odour, or tasted a flavour, or felt a touch, or cognised an idea, and if greed, hate or delusion are in him, he knows; "Ther is in me greed, hate, delusion", "and if greed, hate, delusion are not in him, he knows "there is not in me greed, hate, delusion",this is the way by which the meditator succeeds in achiveing emancipation, even if he is devoid of any sort of faith or religious inclination or acceptance of any hearsay, or specious reasoning or delight in dogmas.[10]

V. The Age-Old Techniques : *Ānāpāna* and *Vipassanā*

We have given a brief survey of the practice of *Samatha* and *Vipassanā* as described in the Pāli scriptures. In modern times, we meet with a new method that is called *Sukkha Vipassanā*, that is, *Vipassanā* bereft of the *Samatha* practice of *Jhāna*. We find in ancient texts, as already noted, *samatha* preceded by *Vipassanā,* which means that the penetrative insight into reality is followed by the entry into the stages of absorption (*samādhi*), as well as the usual sequence of *Samatha* followed by *Vipassanā*. In the absorptions, the mind attains a very high degree of concentratiion, purity and calm and reaches deep down into the subconscious and the unconscious, the store-house of the *anusayas* or the latent seeds of defilemenmt. With such a preparation, the subsequent practice of *Vipassanā* succeeds in bringing quicker results. But the conditions necessary for cultivating absorptions are difficult to achieve in modern society and as such the modern mind is naturally more attracted by the direct practice of *Vipassanā*. It may be mentioned here that the *Ānāpānasati*, as an important constituent of *Samatha* is only a means to an end, and cannot independently lead to the highest goal of liberation which is attained only through *Vipassanā*. In fact, *Ānāpānasati* is very intimately connected with *Vipassanā*, as it lies on the borderland of *Kāyānupassanā* with which the *Vipassanā* begins. In the *Paṭisambhidāmagga*, in connection with the exposition of *Ānāpānasati*, it is said :

imehi navahi ākārehi dīgham assāsa-passāsā kayo, upaṭṭhānam sati, anupassanā ñālaṃ; kayo upaṭṭhān{ṃ, no sati; sati upaṭṭhānaṃ ceva sati ca; tāya satiyā, tena ñāṇena taṃ kāyam anupassati; tena vuccatikāye kāyānupassanāsatipaṭṭhāna-bhāvanā.[11]

The inhaling and exhaling is the *Kāya, upaṭṭhānaṃ* is (of) the *sati, anupassanā* is knowledge; the *Kāya* is *upaṭṭhāna,* and not *sati*; the *sati* is *upaṭṭhāna* as well as *sati*; by that *sati,* by the knowledge, he (the meditator) sees the *kāya*; therfore, it is said that the *bhāvanā* (meditation) centred on *Kāya* is called *Kayānupassanā satipaṭṭhāna*. Here it should be noted that mindfulness centred on *kāya* is also extolled as a supreme virtue in the *Aṅguttara Nikāya* in the following words :

> *ekadhamme, bhikkhave, bhāvito bahulīkato mahato saṃvegāya saṃvattati .... mahato yogakkhemaya saṃvattati... katame ekadhammo ? Kāyagatā sati... amataṃ te, bhikkhave, paribhuñjanti ye kayagatāsatiṃ paribhuñjanti.*
>
> One thing, monks, if developed and constantly practised, couduces to great thrill... to the fruits of the life of a recluse (*yogakkhema*). What is that one thing ? It is mindfulness centred on body... they who parktake of mindfulness centred on body do indeed partake of the Deathless (*amataṃ* that is, *Nibbāna*).[12]

The *Ānāpānasati* and the *Vipassanā* qua *kāyānupassanā* are thus age-old techniques for the achivement of mental peace and moral purification.

References

1. *Aṅguttara Nikāya* vol. I. p. 58 (Nalanda)

   dve me, bhikkhave, dhammā vijjābhāgiyā. katame dve samatho ca viapssanā ca. samatho, bhikkhave, bhāvito kathamanubhoti ? cittaṃ bhāvīyati, cittaṃ bhāvitaṃ kathamanubhoti ? yo rāgo so pahīyati. Vipassnā, bhikkhave, bhāvitā kathamanubhoti pañña bhāviyati ?. paññā bhāvitā kathamanubhoti ? yā avijja sā pahīyati. rāgupakkilitthaṃ vā, bhikkhave, cittaṃ na vimuccati, avijjupakkilitthaṃ vā paññā na bhavīyati; iti kho, bhikkhave, rāgavirāgā ceto-vimutti, avijjāvirāgā paññāvimutti.

2. *Saṃytta Nikāya* Vol. III.p. 174, (Nalanda)

3. *Paṭisambhidāmagga* p. 25 (Nalanda)

   avikkhepaṭṭhena samatho abhiññeyo; anupassanaṭṭhena vipassanā abhiññeyā; ekarasaṭṭhena samatha-vipassanā abhiññeyā; anativattanaṭṭhena yuganaddhaṃ abhiññeyaṃ.

4. *Aṅguttara Nikāya*, Vol. II, p. 166 (Nalanda)

5. Some of the definitions of *Satipaṭṭhāna* are as follows:

(i) *tesu tesu ārammaṇesu akkhanditvā pakkhanditvā upaṭṭhānato paṭṭhāaṃ sati yeva paṭṭhānaṃ satipaṭṭānaṃ - Visuddhimagga Mahātikā* (Burma), pp. 481-490.

(ii) *sampayutta -dhammesu pamukhā padhānā hutvā kāyādisu ārammaṇesu titthanti, nanarammaṇesu cittagamanaṃ nivattetvā tesveva kāyādisu cit-*

tanibandhana vasena pavattantīti paṭṭhānāni. Sati eva paṭṭānaniti satipaṭṭhānāni - Paramathudipani (Burmese Edition), p.304.

(iii) *Paṭṭhātīti paṭṭhānaṃ asubhagahaṇādivasena anupavisitvā kāyādi-ārammaṇe pavattatīti attho. sati eva paṭṭhānaṃ satipaṭṭhānaṃ Vibhānī* (Burmese Edition), p. 171.

(iv) *Taṃ pana kāya-vedanā-citta-dhammesu asubha dukkha anicca anattākāraggahaṇavasena subha-sukha-nicca-attasaññā-vipallāsa pahāna vasena ca catubbidhaṃ ti vuttaṃ cattāro satipaṭṭhānā ti. Idem.*

6. *Dīgha Nikāya* Vol. II p. 217 (Nalanda)

7. *Aṅguttara Nikāya* Vol. IV, pp. 91-93 (Nalanda)

The Five *nīvaraṇas* are : *Kāmacchanda, byāpāda, thīamiddha, uddhaccakukkuca* and *vicikicchā*. The five *kāmagunas* are : *rūpa, sadda, gandha, rasa* and *photthabba*. The five *upādānakkhandas* are *rūpa, vedana, saññā, sankhāra* and *viññaṇa*. The five *orambhāgiyas* are : *sakkāyadiṭṭhi, vicikicchā, sīlabbataparāmāsa, kāmacchanda* and *byāpāda*. The five *uddhambhāgiyas* are : *rūparāga, arūparāga, māna, uddhca* and *avijja*.

8. *Majjhima Nikāya* Vol. III, p. 144 (Nalanda).

9. *Saṃyutta Nikāya* Vol. II. p. 185 (Nalanda)

10. *Ibid*, pp. 125-128

11. *Paṭisambhidāmagga* p. 205 (Nalanda)

12. *Aṅguttara Nikāya*, Vol. I pp. 42-45.

X

A Survey of Samatha Meditation

Hammalava Saddhatissa

There are two categories of Buddhist meditation. They are known as '*Samatha*' which means the development of calm and concentration, and '*vipassana*' which is the development of insight.

Samatha meditation subjects are FIXED objects which may be internal or external. At the beginning especially if one is working without a teacher, external subjects are perhaps the more suitbale. Possibly the best known and most frequently practised of the external *samatha* meditation subjects are the four colour *kasiṇas*. The practice of *kasiṇa* meditation involves first constructing one's *kasiṇa* and the ancient meditation manuals explain the exact quality and tone of the stipulated colours. They show also how the would-be meditator should fashion his *kasiṇa*. As with the much later Tea cermonies and Zen flower arrangement, the preparation of the *kasiṇa* should be very much part of the meditation itself. Every action should be carried out with quiet awareness and fixed precision. The size may vary : some say that the diameter should measure the same as the hand span of the meditator plus the width of our fingers : others say that the size of the *kasina* should be modfied according to the degree of concentration present in the meditator ; those of dull concentration using larger discs and those whose concentration is sharper may use smaller ones.

The disc is set up at a reasonable distance from the

meditator. Here, again, the sources differ as to the distances they recommend. About ten to fifteen feet is satisfactory. The centre of the disc should be slightly lower than the horizontal eye level of the meditator when he is seated in front of the *kasiṇa.*

When he has built the *kasiṇa* and placed it in a good position and is seated before it, the meditator starts his meditation. The gaze should focus on the disc without staring or straining the vision at all. After a few seconds, the eyes are closed but the concentration remains fixed on the memory of the disc. If a disc appears whilst the eyes are closed, as when we look at the moon for a second and then close but the concentration remains fixed on the memory of the disc. If a disc appears whilst the eyes are closed, as when we look at the moon for a second and then close our eyes - the meditator should concentrate on that until it fades. The process is then repeated until it fades. The process is then repeated unitl the allotted time for the meditation session is over. Sometimes the meditator will find that he can hold the image of the disc much longer than at other times. This should be noted and after some experience it will be found that it is possible to relate the various states and sequences of one's meditation session to one's habits and character traits.

A more elaborate from of *kasiṇa* meditation is the *maṇḍala*. A *maṇḍala* is a symmetrical pattern which is used as an aid to concentration in much the same way as the *kasiṇa*. *Maṇḍalas* are generally many coloured and often show symbolic or mythological figures arranged in an intricate and stylized pattern. Many of the Indian and Tibetan works of art which are on display in the West at the moment were made as *maṇḍalas* and were used by monks in their meditation practices.

But it is '*ānāpānasati*' which is the most respected Buddhist practice and, indeed, this was the meditation used by the Buddha on the night of his Enlightenment when he saw things as they really are. *Ānāpānsati* is the mindfulness of in-breathing and out-breathing and it is a universal meditation subject. It is recommended as a character-correcting practice and it is one of the foremost *samatha* (calming) subjects and it is perhaps the most natural - if that word is understood correctly - and not the most spectacular - of meditation subjects.

The meditator is asked to focus his attention at the tip of the nostrils. It is not necessary to 'squint' (mentally) and focus the closed eyes on the nostrils instead; the closed eyes can be directed in a relaxed manner straight ahead and it is the mind or consciousness which is 'focussed' on the tip of the nostrils. It is sometimes found useful to count the breaths as this may help to anchor the concentration. Various methods of concentration by counting may be used. Usaully it is not recommended to count beyond ten, and if the concentration is broken, the meditator should begin again at one. It is essential to remember that it is not the counting of the breath which matter but the continuity of the concentration on the breath. As with the *kasiṇa* practice, the meditator practising *ānāpānasati* should carefully observe everthing which happens during the meditation session : whether the in-breath or the out-breath is clearer : whether this remains constant throughout the session or whether there is a change in the pattern : whether the concentration is keener at the beginning or at the end of the practice and so on.

Finally, we should also mention the practice of repeating a word or a sequence of words. This sort of practice will be familiar to those who know the meditation systems of the Greek Orthodox Church. The 'Jesus prayer' or 'prayer of the heart' is much used by monks of the Greek Orthodox faith.

With all the differnet forms of *samatha* meditation the chosen subject, whether it be the *'mantra'* or word or pharase, the *maṇḍala* or *kasiṇa* or the very breathing itself, is only a stepping stone or an aid to concentration. The meditator focuses his attention on the chosen subject until the mind becomes quiet and one-pointed. At this stage, conceptual image (*nimitta*) will arise and this is a 'sign' which appears before the closed eyes. If the meditator was using a *kasiṇa*, then a disc may arise eventually. If it was *ānāpānasati*, then there may be a wisp or smoke or a flurry of clouds. If the utterance was used (e.g. '*arahaṃ sammāsambuddho* - free from all impurity, by his own efforts completely enlightened) was being repeated, then the resultant '*nimitta*' may be a vision of a Buddha statue or painting. Or, if a *maṇḍala* containing an image of Christ was used, then the '*nimitta*' might be a picture of that same Christ. A *nimitta* arises when a certain degree of concentration has been achieved - a sort of *vipāka* of a *kammic* development. Anyone, once he has carried out the necessary preparatory work can 'see visions and dream dreams' without supernatural assistance. Indeed, Buddhism recognises no divine intervention in the case of such visions.

Once the *nimitta* has arisen before the closed eyes of the meditator and it may take months or years of conscientious practice before this happens — he abandons the previous subject of his *samatha* practice and focuses the mind on the *nimitta* instead. Care must be taken not to chase *nimittas* ! If it seems to be floating up out of sight, remain clam and quiet, and keep the attention focussed on the central point where the *nimitta* first arose. If this is done, it will soon 'float' back into place again. But if one chases it, it will merely disappear out of the roof ! When concentrating on it, one must be careful that one helps the attention but neither too tight nor too loose, and not too tense either. If attention is too slack, we can begin to observe the *nimitta* closely — its exact colour, texture, size, shape, whether it is increasing or decreasing in size, etc. If the mind is too tense, we should let it rest in the centre of the *nimitta*.

There are three main benefits to be derived from *samatha* meditation. Firstly the meditator will find that some of the calm and concentration attained during his daily meditation session will carry over into the rest of the day. The problems of life will not, of course, have been solved, but he will begin to feel more capable of dealing with them.

As a central point of tranquillity begins to be established in him, he will find that he is endowed with a new sense of proportion and perspective. Fears, disappointments, irritations, hopes, surprises and shocks will not cease to affect him but their impact will be cushioned by his inner calm and he will be less likely to be goaded by them into untimely speech or action. If the meditator notices that his meditation sessions are improving dramatically - he is attaining trance like states of concentration - and yet there is no change in his daily life itself - he should be very wary and examine carefully the content and quality of his meditation sessions. It may well be that what he has been calling tranquility and concentration is in fact a state of self induced hypnotism. The latter, though interesting as a mental phenomenon, has no place in the context of Buddhist meditation nor is it of value to those seeking an answer to the problems of human malaise.

The other two benefits are much more difficult to attain. We could call them (i) ecstatic trances and (ii) miracles.

An ecstatic trance or *jhāna* has been analysed and systematized by Buddhist scholars and its stages have been recognised and named. We shall outline here the sequence of events which precede the attainment of the first *jhāna* (the most elementary first ecstatic trance); this same sequence is then repeated on a higher plane of consciousness as the various stages of *jhāna* are traversed. Firstly, the thought processes are regulated until they revolve around a single theme. The revolutions are narrowed down and the thought remains focussed on the central point. From this stage onwards there is a dropping of conceptual thought in favour of pure awarencess - experience rather than varbalisation. There is an acute sense of pleasurable interest that is gradually refined. Joy arises and quiet happiness. The mind becomes completely one-pointed, free from all division, conflict and confusion and finally there is a breakthrough to another sphere of consciousness known to Buddhists as the first *Jhāna* and to Christians as an ecstatic trance. The attainment of *jhāna* brings a state of unparalleled bliss, the effects of which can be felt in life for some time afterwards. We shall now consider the Buddhist attitude to what Christians would call 'miracles' - walking on water, levitation and the like. Experience tells us that this is nothing to do with divine intervention but the natural outcome of a certain type of human development. Buddhist meditation manuals list the various psychic powers (*iddhis*) towards which the *samatha* meditator can, if he wish, work, Specific subjects are recommended for developing specific 'miraculous' power. As a prerequisite, the meditator has to become thoroughly proficient in the various *jhānas*, be able to enter them at will and in whatever order he chooses. The metitator is warned of the dangers of such achievements - he must not boast of them or show them to others (unless within the community of monks). Christ knew that faith induced by miracles is not ture faith and that his followers must come to him by the slow way of their own experience.

Similarly it is in accord with the warning expressed in meditation manuals - not to use psychic power for one's own personal satisfaction or gratification - that Christ rejected the temptation to turn stone into bread.

The results, both spectacular and intimate, of *samatha*, meditation, raise many questions and doubts in the mind of the meditator. How long can a man live in the blissful *jhāna* world when the basic problems of human suffering has not been solved ? How deeply can one go into the wonders of psychic power without falling captive to its dangers ? The temptation to use meditation experiences for personal, politcal or 'religious' end rather than just observing them as indications that one has attained a high degree of concentration - this temptation is hard to overcome. Christ's third temptation was that of political power — by the annals of the Churches it is recorded that there are many examples of Christian zealots who were a lot less careful than their founder.

For the true follower of the Buddha, the ability to perform miracles and see visions is but a side product of meditation: it may be gratifying and pleasurable but it does not lead one nearer to the goal which is release from the cause of suffering. The branch of Buddhist meditation which deals with this is the development of insight or *vipassanā*.

XI

Insight (vipassanā)

Bhikkhu Nāgasena

Generally speaking, the Buddha's way to ultimate freedom comprises as corner stones Virtue, Concentration and Insight. Buddhaghosa in his celebrated 'Path of Purification' has explained these three categories in terms of Seven Purifications, Insight consisting of five kinds of Purification. Virtue, Concentration and Insight or the Seven Purifications are not levels or stages in the strict sense of the word; they are otherwise called the Noble Eightfold Path or the Three-fold Training. When all constituent parts of the path of training are present and are actually put into practice, this path can be consiaered as the Path Leading to the Cessation of Suffering.

All these aspects of the Path have variously been grouped by the Buddha in many ways according to the needs of individual aspirants. The most important groupings are seven in terms of the Four Applications of Mindfulness, the Four Right Efforts, etc.-the so-called Thirty seven Wings of Enlightenment. These Thirty seven Wings constitute the pristine pure *Abhidhamma,* the Higher *Dhamma,* of the Buddha ; for he calls them the *Dhammas* taught with Highter Knowledge.[1] This *Abhidhamma* is so immortant that according to the Buddha a dispute about any other aspect of his teachting is insignificant compared to this one.[2]

Here we are going to explain the whole practice under one single term, i.e. *Vipassanā,* Insight. Those familiar with Buddhist texts may question why not also talk about

Tranqullity, *Samatha*. In the scriptures *Samatha* and *Vipassanā* are mostly mentioned together. On what score then have we Vipassanā Centres and not Samatha Centres or *Samatha-Vipassanā* Centres? The reason is obvious ; *Vipassanā* is something typical as to the Buddha's way of practice, something new, unheard of before the Buddha's Enlightenment. As for *Samatha* alone, even before the Buddha people could attain the highest level of it by tranquillizing their minds up to the so-called Eighth state of Neither-Perception-Nor-Non-Perception. But spiritual giants got stuck here grasping at such states of mind as being permanent and the essence of their being, Self, Soul, or permanent, abiding entity. The Buddha declared such states of tranquillity to be something conditioned, hence impermanent and non-self. He advised to go further and have insight into their impermanence and insubstantiality–and that is what is called *Vipassanā*. Attainment of peace, calm or tranquillity at any level without having insight into impermanence and nonself is not the ultimate aim of *Buddhadhamma*. Why? Simply because such peace is conditioned and subject to change. Upon this score Insight or *Vipassanā* is generally much more stressed than *Samatha,* although both go together in their "ordinary sense". At times, however, the Buddha simply says *Samatha* is the way to the Unconditioned State.[3] It should be understood that *Samatha* at such place implies the tranquillity of mind accompanied by Insight.

Before we go on to explain *Vipassanā*, it would not be out of place to say a few words about *Samatha*. The Buddha himself never said a word about various kinds or levels of *Samatha,* but if we read between the lines of different discourses, we can see that there are two kinds of *Samatha*. On the one hand the Buddha uses this term in the "ordinary sense" of tranquillity, that is, just an unwavering state of mind at any level. Then he uses the term in the specifiic sense of not only attaining *Jhānas* or Absorptions, but also gaining mastery over them. For instance, he says to attain the Cessation of Perception and Feeling (*Saññāvedayita-nirodha*) two *dhammas*, namely *Samatha* and *Vipassanā* are needed.[4] Here *Samatha* means mastery over the so-called four material and four immateial absorptions without which attainment of Cessation of Perception and Feeling is not feasible. In its specific sense, too, *Samatha* referes to a way of developing Super-natural powers or achieving para-psychological phenomena such as thought reading, all of which, however, are insignificant as far the realization of the Unconditioned or *Nibbāna* is concerned. It seems strange that a person who has attained *Nibbāba* may or may not have supernatural powers; he who has all sorts of supernatural powers does not necessarily attain *Nibbāna*. This is why in *Vipassanā* Centres *Samatha* in its specific sense is belittled and *Vipassanā* emphasized. This atitude may be justified if one recognizes the fact that many people having got some sort of mental power grasp at it and delude themselves and others that they are enlightened or perfect. Anyhow, it should always be remembered that *Samatha* in its "ordinary sense" is very essential. Moreover, *Samatha* in its "ordinary sense" coupled with *Vipassanā* involves the Absorptions which just come about naturally, or unintentionally and which therefore guarantee no super-natural powers. Absorptions involved in *Samatha* in its specific sense are produced with intentional effort and one has gained mastery over them unlike the former. Thus we see that an initiate can have absorptions and develops Insight while dwelling in the absorptions. The Buddha mentions how Venerable Sāriputta, for instance had Insight into the thoughts, rapture, etc. which are the factors of the First Absorption, etc. as being impermanence, arising and ceasing.[5] We may point out here that the accepted opinion that to develop Insight one has to dwell in Access Concentration (*Upacāra-samādhi*) and not in Full Concentration (*Appanāsamādhi*) involving the Absorptions is not valid in the light of the above-mentioned words of the Buddha.

To round up these introductory remarks, it has to be taken for granted that when one develops Insight, Tranquillity in its "ordinary sense" is always developed along with it.

Now we come to the main subject of developing Insight. What is Insight? The wellknown answer iş to see all conditioned things as impermanent, unsatisfactory and non-self. How do we achieve that? By developing Mindfulness (*Sati*) and Full Attention (*Sampajañña*). The Master once summarized his teaching in one sentence by saying, "O brethen, be mindful and fully attentive—that is what I have to teach you."[6] From the practical point of view mindfulness and full attention are synonymous. They are like two wheels of the same vehicle. Talking about Venerable Nanda's mindfullness and attention, the Buddha says : "Knowing the feelings, perceptions and thoughts arise, stay and cease with him."[7] Elsewhere he also says the same thing with regard to mindfulneşs and full attention[8] exclusively. Generally speaking the Master refers to his whole system of practice with regard to a single term, namely, mindfulness; we have hundreds of discourses dealing with the four Applications of Mindfulness.

How do we practice mindfulness ? We have to apply it to the body, to feelings, to mind and to mind-elements. What is the gist of the whole practice ? It consists in knowing and "seeing" feeling ; for all phenomena are (in some way or other) felt or "sensed", that is, they are experienced through feeling (All phenomena gather together in feeling).[9] For our purpose, we shall henceforth use the term sensation ; for in the dictum that all phenomena gather together in feeling, the term phenomena refers to all things, both material and mental, including feeling in its normal sense. In other words "all phenomena" means all the so-called five aggregates (form, feelings, perceptions, tendencies of mind, consciousness) or the very four things which mindfulness is to be applied to. This means is being mindful of body or feelings, mind or mind-elements, one is to be mindful of sensation in each case. This is why the gist of the whole practice is to "see" the feeling or sensation. This is a very crucial point. One should bear in mind that the kind of sensation we are concerned with here is not an ordinary feeling. When the Buddha says that *Nibbāna* is the supreme happiness (*Nibbānam paraman sukham.*) he is not referring to happy or pleasant feeling in its ordinary sense. Although he uses the word happiness (*sukha*) which generally refers to feeling, its use in connection with *Nibbāna*, however, has nothing to do with feeling per se. Words are mere symbols of things and of what we think, feel, conceive, or experience. This is why sometimes one word is used in differnet senses and differnt words are used synonymously. Thus when the Enlightened One says, "All phenomena are experienced through feeling (or gather together in feeling)", he is using the ordinary word feeling in not quite an ordinary sense. But again this different sense is not totally exclusive of the ordinary one. Sensation and ordinary feeling are like water and waves respectively. Waves are water, forms of water. Developing Insight is like diving into the deep water of sensation. This different sense of the feeling in question becomes evident in these words of the Buddha:

"*To the person having feeling, O brethern, do I declare, Suffering, the Cause of Suffering, the Cessation of Suffering and the Way leading to the Cessation of Suffering.*"[10]

How is sensation to be experienced ? By being mindful of the movement of our body, our limbs including breathing; by being mindful of the feeling arising resulting from the contact of the six sense organs with the six corresponding sense objects ; by being mindful of differnet states of mind, and finally by being mindful of mind-elements. One among Thai *Vipassanā* teachers, Ācāriya Dhammadharo[11] has developed a simple way of introducing one to this sensation. Just move your hand (*Saminjite pasarite*) slowly at intervals and fix your mindfulnes at the middle of your palm. Take special note when you begin to start moving the hand and when you stop moving it. After some time you will begin to feel a slight sensation some where in hand, or in the middle, at the back or side of the palm, or in the fingers. As you go on practising, the sensation will gradually become clearer and you will feel it in your whole arm and then elsewhere in your body. You will feel the sensation in your feet as you walk and stand, at the point of bodily contact as you sit or lie down, in your tongue and neck as you move, in the cavities of your body as you pass stool or vrine. As you advance in practice you will experience sensation in your eye-balls, as the light-waves make them vibrate, in your nose, tongue, or anywhere in your body as some object touches it or when any limb moves even a little bit, for instance, the opening and shutting of the eye-lids or a slight movement of the eye-balls. You can experience the whole body as you sit still because air always touches it from outside and the breath inside "fans" every cell of the body. At the sixth sense, the heart-base you can experience sensation as the mental defilements, attachment, aversion and delusion arise and also when they do not arise.

Applying yourself to the practice of experiencing sensation you have to watch closely *(Anupassanā)* its arising and ceasing, from "moment to moment". This is an important point. Arising is not merely the starting of sensation with initial contact and ceasing is not just the stopping of the last contact between organ and stimulus. So long as the contact remains, in between its initial and last impact, you have to contemplate the arising and ceasing as well. Normally our senses work like a movie projector. When the continuity of sense perception is broken into pieces through the practice of contemplation, cherished views of entity and identity vanish, and non-self is realized. In the discourse on the Four Applications of Mindfulness the Master says the meditator contemplates the arising, ceasing and arising-cum-ceasing. The term arising-cum-ceasing seems to be superfluous. It is not. It is on the contrary very significant. It refers to change in the state of "staying". In the scriptures it is clearly stated that the arising ceasing and change of the staying of the five aggregates is evident.[12]

Vipassanā is concerned with the knowledge of pleasant feelings and unpleasant feelings in general and with neither-pleasant-nor-unpleasant or neutral feelings in particular. "In order to know the three kinds of feeling, brethren, develop the Four Applications of Mindfulness,[13] says the Buddha.

For the ordinary man a pleasant feeling is feeling, an unpleasant feeling, is also feeling, but a neither-pleasant-nor-unpleasant feeling does not appear to be a feeling. In case of the third kind of feeling he does not take it to be a feeling at all. He just takes it o be a negative state, the absence of the frst two types of feeling. This is why the Enlightened One says that while greed or lust is due to pleasant feelings and hatred or anger due to unpleasant feelings, delusion or spiritual blindness is due to neither-pleasant-nor-unpleasant feelings. This third kind of feeling is the actual presence of neutral feelings which can be felt or "seen" or rather experienced as something veritable. (Hence in the Pali Text Society's Pali-English dictionary the translation of *Upekkhā* as "zero point between joy and sorrow" is not satisfactory). However, one cannot know that one is feeling the third type of feeling unless one experiences it momentary arising and ceasing. Here the knowledge of "sensation" becomes significant. Men of practice before the Buddha knew the first two kinds of, feeling, but were ignorant of the third. This is why once the Buddha said that only he knows and "sees" feeling among the various contemporary teachers.

Whatever he may have achieved, he who says, "I am above likes and dislikes." May still be an ordinary worlding, a deluded man, for he may be attached to neutral feeling. In the *Salāyatanavibhanga-sutta* (*Majjhima N. Sutta* No. 137) the Buddha has this to say : "Here in what are the six neutral feelings connected with worldly life ? When a foolish, *arahant*, average person has seen a form with the eye, there arises the neutral feeling of an uninstructed average person who has not conquered his limitations (of defilements), who has not conquered the consequences (of defilements), who does not see peril (in neutral feeling)—neutral feeling such as this does not overcome form. Therfore this is called neutral feeling connected with worldly life—(the same applies to sound, etc., the remaining five sense objects). Herein what are the six neutral feelings connected with renunciation? When one has had insight into the impermanence of all forms, into their alteration, disappearance and arrest and knows, 'formerly as well as now all these forms are impermanent, painful, subject to alteration' from seeing this thus as it realy is by means of perfect wisdom, neutral feeling arises. Neutral feeling as this overcomes forms. Therefore this is called neutral feeling connected with renunciation—(the same applies to sounds, etc., the remaining five sense objects)." Here we should note that when one sees or realizes impermanence and alteration of the changing of forms, sounds, etc., from moment to moment, the change of feeling or sensation is also seen. In the light of this passage quoted here it is clear as to how an ordinary worldling and a wise man differ in their experience of neutral feeling.

Some people think 'pleasure' or to be elated is one end and 'displeasure', or to be depressed is another extreme. They get attached to neutrality regarding it as the middle way. The Buddha, however has to say this : "The wise man who knowing the two extremes (of pleasant and unpleasant feelings) does not get stained by the middle (neutral feeling)—him I call a great man ; for he in this world overcomes the seamstress, craving."[14] So be careful lest you get stained by neutrality.

Elsewhere the Buddha says a man of practice, having seen form (likewise the remaining sense objects perceived by their corresponding sense organs) with the eye, neither gets depressed nor elated and being neutral, mindful and recollected or attentive he leads his life.[15] Herein take note of the terms "mindful" and "recollected". He is not just netural, but with being neutral he is also mindful and recollected. This being maindful and recollected refers to his being aware of impermanence or the momentary arising and ceasing of the neutral feeling. This awareness of impermanence, does, of course, also refer to pleasant and unpleasant feeling. But as one can "normally experience" these two kinds of feeling and is easily prone to be unaware of neutral feeling, the expression "mindful and recollected" has especially been mentioned with regard to the latter

This is also the case, because in our daily life we have far more periods of undergoing neutral feeling than any other.

Some people have been heard saying that so long as one "sees" movement or impermanence of things, or so long as one's mind is "seen" in movement or as impermanent, one has no peace of mind. They declare the mind must be stilled and unmoved. They even go so far as to say that the mind which is in movement, arising and ceasing, were not the genuine mind. They are thus blinfolded getting entrapped in the view of an unchanging entity or soul. They do not know that as a matter of fact there can be "real peace' only in movement and "real stillness' only in arising and ceasing. As a technical term this fact is referred to as unification or yoking together *(Yuganaddha)* of Tranquillity and Insight *(Samatha-Vipassanā)*. The static aspect of mind, tranquillity refers to *samatha,* the insight into the arising and ceasing, the dynamic aspect of mind, referes to *vipassanā*. This unity has successfully been illustrated in a Zen drawing of Bodhidharma with his face and body perfectly calm, whereas his robe is fluttering in the wind. A monk comes to Buddha and indirectly declares his attainment of *Arahantship* : .... "In the same way as one solid rock cannot be shaken by wind, thus all forms, tastes, sounds, smells, touches and agreeable as well as disagreeable states do not have a hold on the mind of a 'perfect one', because his mind has won freedom and is unshakable while he (continually) sees (the arising and) ceasing of mind.[16] In this passage we see that the mind is spoken of as freed and stilled or unshakable. But being still does not meant permanent or unchanging. What is meant may be illustrated with the help of a simile : Not exposed to wind, a flame remains unmoved and does not flicker. On the other hand one cannot conceive of a flame which is still but not burning, the same applies to mind as being serene and calm or unshakable, but bereft of its nature of arising and ceasing. The flame itself implies burning, so does mind is unruffled refers to its being unshaken in the face of all stimuli from without. That the mind is in motion refers to its very nature of arising and ceasing.

Having discussed mind let us not forget about the importance of the body. Generally speaking, from the practical point of view the body ought to be considered first. This is why in the Four Applications of Mindfulness the body is dealt with first. The Buddha uses in connection with the body such adjectives as *Salāyatanikam*, "of six sense bases" thereby including the mind-base in it. Not only that all the four Noble Truths of Suffering, the Cause of Suffering, Cessation of Suffering, and the Way leading to the Cessation of suffering, are declared by him to be in this fathom long frame-work of body with perception and mind. So first to experience one's body will naturally lead to experiencing one's mind. If you want to see the 'mind-king' you have to enter the city of the body. But how do you enter it ? By opening the door of "sensation" by means of using your hand, e.g. when taking up your practice of meditation as explained earlier. Once you have gone through the door of "sensation", you will perceive different things in the city, at different places, for instance, the "T.V. station" in the eye, the "radio station" in the ear, and finally you will be able to see the king.

It has been alleged that Buddhism is a very profound and comprehensive teaching. But remember no matter how profound and comprehensive it is, it cannot be profounder than what can be experienced withing the length of one's own body–fathom long.

As you have your body always and every where with you, you can develop mindfulness everywhere and at anytime, even at such common places as toilets. The body is one's laboratory. What has been said here is all about the way of using the library or laboratory. But before you will be able to use it you will have to open its door by yourself, the door of sensation. This is the first and foremost requirement you will have to fulfil.

Here it would not be out of place to mention the approach to this sensation, the gate to *Nibbāna*, as has been put forward by *Vipassanā* teachers outside Thailand.

First we mention Thray Sithes-U Ba Khin of Burma. This is how he puts the experience of sensation in question:[17]

"The Buddha made it known to his disciples that the human body is composed of *Kalapas* (atomic units) : each dying out simultaneously as it becomes. *Kalapa* is a mass formed of natural-elements. These *Kalapas* are in a state of perpetual change and flux. They are nothing but a stream of energies, just as the light of a candle or an electric bulb. The body, as we call it, is not an entity, as it seems to be, but a continum of matter with life force co-existing. Does man feel the rocking vibrations within himself ? What will be the reparcussion on the mental attitude of the man who introspectively sees that his own body is mere energy and vibration ? To quench thirst one just easily drinks a glass of water from a villagewell. Supposing his eyes are as powerful as microscopes, he would surely hesitate to drink the very water in which he must be seeing the magnified microbes. So also, when one comes to a realization of the perpetual change within himself (i.e. *Anicca* or impermanence ; he must necessarily come to the understanding, as a sequal there to, of the vibration and friction of the atomic units within and without. By introspective meditation he makes analytical study of nature, firstly, of *Rūpa* (Matter) and then of *Nāma* (mind and mental properties). He feels — and then also he sees the *Kalapas* in their true state."

"The 'Truth of Suffering' is something which must be experienced before it can be understood. For example, we all know from science that everything that exists is nothing but vibration caused by the whirling movement of infinite numbers of electrons ; but how many of us can convince themselves and accept the fact — that our own bodies are subject to the same law. Why not then try to feel as to what the body is so far as it is related to ourselves ? Why not try to feel as they (electrons) really are so far as they to your goodself ?"

"With developed mental power, one can see through

and through more than what one can see with the help of the latest scientific instruments."

"The extract from a diary of one of my disciples which I will presently read out will give you an idea of what suffering within is. Here it goes:-

"21.8.51. No sooner began I to meditate, when I felt as if someone is boring a hole through my head and I felt the sensation of crawling ants all over my head. I wanted to scratch it, but my Gurū forbade me to do it. Whithin an hour I saw the sparkling radiance of blue light tinged with violet colour gradually entering my body. When I lay in my room continually for three hours I almost fell unconscious and felt a terrible shock in my body. I was about to be frightened out of my wits but my Gurū encouraged me to proceed. I felt my whole body heated up and I also felt an indication of the electronic needle at every part of my body.

"22.8.51. Today I laid down meditating for nearly three hours. I had a sensation of feeling that my whole body was in flame and I also saw sparkles of blue and violet rays of light moving from top to bottom aimlessly. Then my Gurū told me that the changing in my body is "*Anicca*" (impermanence) and the pain and suffering following it is "*dukkha*" and that one must get to a state beyond and that one must get to a state beyond "*dukkha*" or 'suffering'.

"23.8.51. My Gurū asked me to concentrate on my breast without the radiation of light and added that we are reaching the state of "philosophy of our body." I did accordingly and came to the conclusion that our body is full of "suffering".

"What is man ? Man is after all mental forces personified. What is matter ? Matter is nothing but mental forces materialized, a result of the re-action of the moral (positive) and immoral (negative) forces. Buddha said '*cittena niyate loko*'—"the world (negative forces. Buddha said 'cittena niyate loko'—"the world is mind-made."

So far the extract from "What Buddhism Is" by Thray Sithes U Ba Khin. Before we mention the approach of another teacher, also from Burma, it may be added, that unlike realising sensation through a particular movement of one's hand first, mentioned before, U Ba Khin starts contemplating breathing and realises sensation at the spot of contact of breath.

Secondly we will here mention the approach of Sunlun Gakyaung Sayadaw as a disciple describe it in "*The Yogi And Vipassanā*"

(According to his method, too, the contemplation of breathing, notably strong breathing is started with)[18] :

"Mental noting tends to take place at a much slower pace than the actual process of phenomena. Thus instead of being able to see these processes as they are, there is the tendency to keep slipping into a past where the processes are reconstructed by an intervening reasoning mind. To be able to keep up with the natural processes, the *yogi* needs only be mindful. This is not difficult to perform. The initial requirement is awareness of sensation. Be aware of touch or sensation or mental phenomena. Watch and guard this awareness of sensation with mindfulness. When the awareness of sensation is guarded with mindfulness, thoughts are locked out, they cannot intrude. No opportunity is offered for formation of concepts, images or ideas to arise. Thereby the processes are got at directly in the very moment of occurrence as they are in themselves without the distortation of thought. This is true *Vipassanā*.

"Of the four methods of *ānāpānasati* (mindfulness of breathing) the first three are (pure) *samatha* exercisses. According to the first method there is counting (one normally counts 1 to 10 while breathing in and 1 to 10 as one breathes out). Numbers are concepts. Form is an image. According to third method the going in and out of breath is noted. This is achieved through the creation of ideas. Concepts images and ideas belong to the sphere of conventional truth, as they are conceived by us, but not reality itself. Only the fourth method where the sense of touch alone is taken in its bareness, involves *Vipassanā*. Yet even this practice can go astray if one handles touch or sensation with the gloves of concepts and ideas. If instead of being aware of the touch in its bare actuality, if instead of guarding this awareness with mindfulness the *yogi* makes a mental note of it, that momnet he has slipped into the old habit of forming concepts or ideas and therefore he practices *samatha* as exclusive of the intended *vipassanā* practice.

"The motto of Sunlun Sayadaw is : "Be vigorously mindful of the awareness of touch."

"Mindfulness is to be established through rigorous awareness of touch and sensation.

"Insight (*Vipassanā*) is the elimination of concepts (*Paññatti*). Therefore the chief characteristic of the right method should be its power of immediate and direct access to the real. With this power of immediate penetration to the real a man might stop wandering about the surface realm, piling up concept upon concept, while ostensibly pointing to the real. For instance, when touch arises he should be able to grasp the bare fact of touch without any need for formulating the concept, "touch, touch." He should be aware of the precise moment of the occurrence of TOUCH-SENSATION, and his mindfulness should be simultaneously with it. These three events should happen simultaneously-touch, awareness, mindfulness. Reality (of events) is to be grasped at the actual moment of occurrence. If mindfulness cannot be awakened to take place simultanceously with the moment of occurrence because of any interference whatsoever, then reality will have died away, subsided in the interim any consciousness of that past event would be only the result of a glancing back at it, an after-thought. If the bare fact of touch is not grasped mindfully at its precise moment of happening, because the concept, "touch, touch," however swiftly formed, then during that moment of conceptualisation the touch-event would have occurred and ended and whatever else is grasped later can be only a memory, a mentally created image of the touch, replica of the real.

"A right method should not require the prior memorising of a series of formulae or a numerical list of items or mastery of an elaborate theory.

"Discursive knowledge of texts and philophies may well aid the meditator after the event of meditation when he wishes to conceptualise the knowledge of the real he has won in the course of meditation. But, coming before the event, such theoretical studies tend to get in the way of the meditator who has to throw aside concepts and discursive, conventional knowledge to get through to the real.

"Every time he wishes to practise mindfulness of consciousness and mental elements, the *yogi* will have to pass through the stations of touch and sensation, till his mind is throughly cleansed, made firm and serviceable.

"Strong, hard and rapid breathing will cause inhaled friction against the tips of the nostrils, the upper lip or some other part of the body in that region. Be mindful of that touch of breath.

"When the breath touches the nostril tip or upper lip you will be aware of it. Be mindful of that awarness." said Sunlun Sayadaw. Let not a SINGLE TOUCH pass without awareness. Be aware of every single touch.

"Do not let the awareness be that of the breath-body. Do not follow it in and out of the body. Do not follow it in and out of the body. Do not take note of the area of touch of breath, whether it be the nostril or upper lip. Let awareness be only of sensation of touch of breath. Be mindful only of the sensation of touch.

"Fatigue may set in at the early stages of strong, hard, rapid breathing, but the *yogi* neither stops nor reduces the strength and rapidity of breathing. "Don't rest when fatigued," said Sunlun Sayadaw. The fatigue is probably due to either insufficient strength of inhalation or too excessive blowing out of exhalation. The remedy is to increase the strength of inhalation. When the intensity of inhalation and exhalation are balanced at a high level, the fatigue will disappear.

"Sunlun Sayadaw requires direct, immediate contact with reality. The time and effort required first to build a conceptual bridge to approach reality cannot be afforded. Confornted with the elephant of one's search, one does not follow the footprints backwards, and then retrace them again to the elephant. When there arises an ache one has immediately to catch hold of the fact of the ache ; one must not formulate the concept, "aching, aching" and then return to the fact of the ache. Therefore the meditator is advised: Avoid giving names, do not conceptualise "reality".

"Neither anticipate sensation nor reflect on it. Be mindful of the sensation in the immediacy of its arising or vanishing which is in the present, the now.

"When his mind has penetrated sensation, the meditator will no longer feel the form of his foot, or arm or body ; he will no longer feel that "I" am suffering. There conceptual notions will be replaced by a simple clear awareness of sensation alone. And because the idea of an "I" which suffers has been removed, the meditator will not feel the discomfort of the unpleasant sensation. The sensation which a few moments ago was felt as pain or burning will now be felt by the meditator *as an intense sensation without the element of infliction.*[19]

"It is possible to overcome unpleasant sensation. Everything being impermanent, it must end sometime. This end can occure in various ways. Its intensity can subside ; but this would not be a true ending. Some measure of unpleasant sensation would remain. The real overcoming of unpleasant sensation takes place *when the meditator dwells in the sensation*, watching the sensation without thinking any thought connected with the sensation ; then it is consumed, it ends, it snaps, it is shed, or extinguished. It is said to be consumed when it gradually subsides till there is no remainder. It ends when the meditator follows it till there is no more of it, like a road followed to the end, like a length of string felt along the whole length till nothing is felt. It snaps when it breaks off suddenly as when a taut rope is snapped. It is shed like the skin of a snake. It is extinguished like a light which has used up its oil and wick.

"In being mindful of unpleasant sensation collect the body and mind together and keep both perfectly still. Watch the unpleasant sensation with bated breath. Hold the breath. Hold the breath as long as one can normally hold it. This is not an exercise in breath retention. It is just the normal practice effected in carrying out the common duties of life. Whenever something is done with great attention the breath is naturally held back. For example, in putting a thread through the eye of a needle the operator naturally holds his breath till the task is accomplished. In the like manner the meditator should watch unpleasant sensations with bated breath. This will enable him to exercise greater awareness and more rigorous mindfulness.

"When the meditator is mindful of the awareness of touch, there is in it the application of mindfulness to the body, sensation, consciousness and to mental constituents. Being mindful of one the meditator is mindful of all the other.

"At no moment of the day will his body not be in contanct of touch. The meditator should be mindful to touch of body against chair, etc. He should if possible be mindful of touch of visual object against eye, touch of sound against ears, of taste against tongue, of smell against nose. "Be rigorously mindful of the awareness of touch.", said Sunlum Sayadaw"

From the above extracts on the approach of U Ba Khin and Sunlun Sayadaw who is regarded by the Burmese as a *Arahant*, the importance of sensation becomes clear. Now we can summarise all that has been said in the following three points :

1. Live in the present. "Do not go after the past ; do not long for the future ; the past has passed away, the future has not yet come. Whatever is in the present, watch it closely here and now, and firmly and steadily pierce it (through wisdom) and develop this state of mind"[20]—says the Buddha.

2. Make the mind "live" with the body, with its sense organs. This is another way of putting the first point. When our mind is not with the body, it is lost in 'time and space' outside.

3. Feel sensation in the body with its sense organs, including the mind-organ. With the contact of sense objects there is always created sensation at the sense organs. This is the sensation created by "motor acts", or activity, or "motor behaviour"—as called by some scientists. This sensation is the sensation of impermanence (*Anicca-paṭisaṁvedi*) or arising and ceasing. It is the sensation of vibration. Every phenomenon is a form of vibration, a process both within and without. Establish your mindfulness on this sensation of vibration, and there is no need to make any note, verbally and mentally. To make a note is like handling an object with hands wearing gloves ; you cannot feel the heat or cold of an object with gloves on. Also make a note that, just to live in the present or to keep the mind with the body will enable you to attain tranquillity alone, as exclusive of Insight. This is why after advising to watch closely what-ever is in the present, here and now, the Enlightened One added, "and firmly and steadily pierce it". This piercing means penetrating or having Insight into its nature of arising and ceasing, from moment to moment. You cannot conceive of a flame without the process of buring. You cannot conceive sensation without its momentary arising and ceasing. The feeling you experience ordinarily without experience of arising and ceasing from moment to moment is not the sensation we have been dealing with here. If you can "see" the momentary process of arising and ceasing within the ordinary feeling, you have

got it. Sensation is inner feeling. This is called "seeing" feeling in feelings ; this is what is called "seeing" the body in the body, mind in the mind and mind-elements in mind-elements. We have a body, but we do not feel it, do not experience it. We have feeling but we do not "see" it. We have our mind, but we do not experience it ; the same is true of mind-elements. But if we have Insight into the sensation of arising and ceasing as explained above, we can feel them, we can see them and "touch" them. We see forms, but we do not experience them (*Rūpapaṭisaṁvedi*); we hear sounds, but we do not experience them (*Sadda-paṭisaṁvedi*) - and the same is true of the other objects. But if we have 'acquainted' ourselves with sensation of arising and ceasing, we can experience them. "In the same way as sheaves are beaten or thrashed by six men with flails in their hands, so are the sense-orgains 'beaten' by the six sense-objects of forms, sounds, etc."[21] says the Buddha. This is literally true. This is not just figurative speech. You can feel the sensation of 'beating' in your eye, etc.

Finally you may like to know the benefit of all this practice. Well, the ultimate benefit is to experience *Nibbāna*, the final Freedom of heart and mind. But as a by-product of practice, even prior to experiencing *Nibbāna,* you can gain many benefits. To mention a few, you can sleep without bad dreams, you need not take pills in order to sleep, you feel relaxed : nervous diseases caused by mental strain are cured ; you can more easily cope with the adversities of life without being depressed.

> The whole world is tormented by words
> And there is no one who does without words
> But in so far as one is free from words,
> Does one really understand words.
>
> —Saraha's Treasury of Songs

References

1. *Majjhima Nikāya Samagama-sutta* : 104 (Dhamma abhiññādesita)

2. Idem

3. *Saṃyatta Nikāya, Asaṁkhata-saṃyutta* 2:1.

4. *Saṃyatta Nikāya. Citta-saṃyutta 6.*

5. *Majjhima Nikāya, Anupada-sutta* : 111.

6. *Saṃyatta Nikāya, Satipaṭṭhāna-saṃyutta* 1:2

7. *Aṅguttara Nikāya, Aṭṭhaka-nipāta Mettā-vagga* , 9

8. *Saṃyatta Nikāya, Satipaṭṭhānasanyutta* 4 : 5

9. *Anguttara Nikāya, Aṭṭhaka-nipāta Mūlaka-sutta (Vedanasamosarañа sabbe dhammā)*

10. Vediyamānassanaṁ bhikkhave dukkhanca paññapemi...... dukkha-nirodha-gamininca paṭipadaṁ.

11. The Vipassanā Centre of Beautiful Fig Trees (Wat Sai-Ngam), Thailand.

12. *Samyatta Nikāya, Khandha-saṁyutta 4(Rūpassa kho avuso uppado paññayati vayo paññayati thitassa aññathattam paññayati.....viññanassa. paññayati.*

13. *Saṁyatta Nikāya, Satipaṭṭhāna-samyuta* 5:9

14. *Aṅguttara Nikāya, Chakka-nipāta* 2 :1 & also *Suttanipāta* -1042

15. *Aṅguttara Nikāya, Chakkha-nipāta paṭhama- paṇṇasa Āhuṇeyya-vagga*-1

16 *Saṃyatta Nikāya. Salāyatan-saṃyutta, Catuttha-paṇṇasa, Asivasa-vagga, Kiṁsuka-sutta.*

17. Adapted from *What Buddhism is ?* by Thray Sithes U Ba Khin.

18. Adapted from "*The Yogi And Vipassanā*"

19. In this statement meaning of "Sensation" as an experience becomes clear—writer's note.

20. *Majjhima Nikāya. Bhaddekaratta-sutta* : 131

21. *Saṃyatta Nikāya, Salāyatana-saṃyutta, Āsivisa-vagga.*

XII
Kāmacchanda : A Nīvaraṇa

Harcharan Singh Sobti

Better it we proceed from where *we are*. And, we are in the clutches of *kāmacchanda* (sensual desire), a *nīvaraṇa* (hindrance) in the way of developing *vipassanā* (Insight). *Kāmacchanda* is just one of the five *nīvaraṇas*. A good amount of energy gets wasted through this channel, alone. So, we have a case against it. We propose to examine the *modus operandi* of *Kāmacchanda* in the background of Theravādā Buddhism.

What is *Kamacchanda* ? the term *kāmacchanda* consists of two word componets : *Kāma* + *chanda*. Subjectively speaking *Kāma* means, "(a) enjoyment, pleasure on occasion of sense, (b) sense-desire."[1] *Chanda* stands for "impulse, excitement, intention, resolution, will, desire for, wish for, delight in."[2] When both the words put together *kāmacchanda* means sensual desire and it is only enlarged term of *kāma*."[3] *Kāmacchanda*, therefore, operates through five channels of sense-organs and manifests itself in equal number of forms viz. vizible, sound, smell, taste and tangible. To add further, these forms can be classified constituting *Kāmacchanda*, only, when these happen to be "agreeable, pleasent, liked, enticing, connected with sensual pleassure, alluring."[4] *kāma* not only dominates over the multifarious activities of human beings, it occupies similar position in Theravada Buddhism, as well. It is placed number one in the scheme of the three *taṇhās*[5] (cravings); three *esanās*[6] (longings) ; the four *upādānas*[7] (attachment) ; the four *āsavās*[8] (intoxicants of mind); the four *oghas*[9] (floods of worldly turbulence) ; the five *nīvaraṇas*[10] (hindrances) ; *Satta Anusuya*[11] and the ten *sanyojanas*[12] fetters etc. And, we are concerned, at the moment, with *Kāma* (or *Kāmacchanda*) as a *nīvaraṇa* in the way of developing *vipassanā*.

When one indulges in the forms 'agreeable' and 'alluring', it does give enjoyment. The repeated performances of sensual-indulgence, in course of time, takes the form of habit and is likened to spider's web. Here, we need to remind ourselves that, "*Sabbe Kāma aniccāti* : the pleasures of senses are transient in nature."[13] The perception of *anicca* (impermanence), naturally, leads one to *anattā* (no-self) and *Dukkha*. When every thing belonging to phenomenal existence is subject to law of flux, *atta* (self) is not at all an exception to it. This realization helps one to drop ego. Again it is through the awereness of the universal phenomenon of impermanence that one learns that the *Dukkha* is an outcome of unsuccessful attempt at manipulating things which are, infact, not things but processes. Also, in order to dispense with sensual plessures, an indulgent one is made to visualize these plessures as (i) *aṭṭhi-kankhala* (a chain of bones) ; (ii) *maṇsapesi* (a piece of decaying flesh); (iii) *angāra-Kāsu* (a pit of glowing cinders) ; (iv) *asisūna* (a slaughter-house) ; (v) *Sappa-Sira* (a Snake's Head)."[14]

Kāmacchanda the first among the pānca *nīvaraṇa* is also described in *Sammaññaphala sutta*[15] by means of a beautiful simlie. When *Kāmacchanda* preys upon a man, the latter, instantly, happens to acquire the psyche of a debter who has failed to payback his contracted loan. Buddhaghosa (5th. A.D.) in *Sumangala Vilasini*[16], a commentary on *Dīghanikāya* has quite convincingly explained the similarity that exists between the mode of behaviour of an undischarged debtor and the lustful being. The point of similarty, however, between them is their capicity to endure. The debtor endures all the possible forms of humiliation at the hands of his creditor. The man overpowered by *Kamacchanda* is by no means less heroic in enduring the similar injuries inflicted upon him, in the course of seeking their gratification. The search for gratification of senual pleasures alongwith its results is beautifully illustated in the *Potalia Sutta,* as under :

> "A butcher throws before a dog tormented by hunger, a bare and fleshless bone with which he can not satisfy his hunger—like such a bare bone are the sensual pleasures, full of torment and Suffering, out of which only evil arise.......... Sensual pleassures are like a beautiful dream-vision, which vanishes when one awakes, like a borrowed treasure on account of which one is envied by those who do not know that it is only borrowing."[17]

The above illustrations make one thing amply clear that the craving for sensual pleasures is sure to lead us astray. Passions, smouldering or boiling, for sensual plessures, are decidedly great hindrances and ought to be extinguished while looking after the spiritual aspect of the Becoming. The one emancipated from the lustful feeling is compared with the debtor who has not only paid back his debt but also earned a surplus for maintenance in future.

So far, we have tried to acquaint ourselves with *Kāmacchanda* operating as a defiling factor that pollutes the human mind. The mind is its primordial form, in Buddhism, is characterized as pure and radiant. The mind gets defiled on account of external impurities.[18] These Impurities are nothing but *nīvaraṇas* in the way of discovering the purity of mind. The mind overwhelmed by sonsual lust is compared to a bowl of water mixed with lac or turmreic or blue or yellow dye, in the following manner:

"Suppose, *brahmin*, a bowl of water mixed with lac or turmeric or blue or yellow dye, and suppose a man with good insight should look closely for the reflection of his own face. *He would not know or see it as it realy is*. Just so, *brahmin*, when one dwells with his heart possessed by sensual lust overwhelmed by sensual lust, and knows not in very truth any refuge from sensual lust that has arisen—at such time he neither knows nor sees in very truth his own profit.........."[19]

Vipassanā meana *'to see things as they realy are'*. The sensuel lust or any *nīvaraṇa* for that matter causes blindness of insight and as a result blurs our frue vision of 'things and beings' *as they are.*

Let us see how *vipassanaā is* aroused following the course formulated by the Buddha. The Buddha in *Mahāsatipaṭṭhana Sutta*[20] of *Dīgha Nikāya* has delineated the path of suppressing *nīvaraṇas* with the aid of *sati* (mindfulness) that straight away observes the bodily and mental phenomenon without having any recourse to the practising of *Jhāna.* The phenomena of corporeal organism, in the instant *sutta*, is divided into four-fold foundations of mindfulness : '*Kaya* (body), *vedaṇā* (feeling), *citta* (state of mind) and *dhamma* (mental objects). The *pañca-nīvaraṇas* fall within the purview of *Dhammānupassanā.* Reqarding *Kāmacchānda* it is stated, thus :

> "Herein, O *Bhikkhu*, a brother when within him is sensuous desire, is aware of it, reflecting : 'I have within me sensuous desire.' or again, when within him is no sensous desire, he is aware of this. And he knows of the uprising of such desire unfelt before, knows too of his putting aside that unrisen sensuous desire, knows too of the non-arising in future of that banished sensuous desire."[21]

As a result of regularly practising mindfulness regarding diverse mental phenomenon, one *discovers* oneself to be a *draṣṭā* (Seer) and views the rise and fall of *Kāmacchanda* from a distance, in a detached manner. There is a beautiful illustration in *Śiva-purāṇa* regarding viewing of *Kāmacchanda* in this detached manner. Let us be familiar with the details of account of '*Kāma's* destruction by *Śiva*,' relevant to our discussion.

Śiva contemplates :

"How is it that obstacles have cropped up while I am performing the great penance ? Who can be that wicked person who has made my mind highly perturbed ?

With love I have described in bad taste another man's woman. I have contravened rules of virtue and transgressed the bounds of the vedas."

"He [Śiva] saw *kāma* stationed on His left side with his bow fully drawn and ready to discharge the arrow. *Kāma* was haughty and so was very senseless.

......Standing high up in the air, holding the arrow and the bow, *kāma* discharged his arrow, usually unerring on Śiva.

The infallible weapon became futlile on the Great Lord. The furious weapon calmed down in regard to the Great Soul, Siva.

Kāma was frightened when his weapen failed. Standing there and seeing Lord Śiva, the conquerer of death in front, he trembled."

"When the gods eulogised thus, a great flame of fire sprang from the third eye of the infuriated Śiva.

That fire orginating instantaneously from the eye in the middle of his forehead blazed with flames shooting up and resembling the fire of final dissolution in refulgence."

"Even before the gods had the time to say ; 'Let him be forgiven, let him be excused,' it reduced *Kāma* to ashes."[22]

The two key-expressions that deserve special attention are 'the third-eye' and 'in the middle of his forehead'. In fact, these two underline single phenomenon. The mind of *puthujana*, using Buddhist terminology, either moves in the past or in the future and *both are not there*. When the mind is brought in the middle *i.e.* in the present, it simply disappears. In this state of no-mind one is *draśṭā* and which is synonymous with the third-eye. The technique of *Vipassanā* when followed diligently, leads to the self-discovery of being *draśṭā*.

The perpetual practice of reviewing the phenomenon of *Kāmacchanda,* as in the instant case, results in deepening the insight or *vipassanā* to such an extent that one actually starts visualising the three phenomenal aspects of existence. The *aniccā* for him is no more a (borrowed) concept. *Aniccā* by way of corraboration helps in visualising *anattā*. Thereafter, it becomes imperative to *see dukkha* as a resultant of clinging to something *which is not there*. This way one qualifies after undergoing a practice of *vipassanā* that may be *kāyanupassanā, vedanānupassanā, cittānupassanā* or *dhammānupasana, to see things as they realy are.*

When the five channels of sense-orgains are plugged with *vipassanā* the leakage of energy is stopped and it is tranaformed into *Karuṇā* (Compassion). *Karuna,* in Buddhist sense, is effected through the transformation of energy, otherwise, wasted while indulging in *Kāmacchanda* or other *nīvarṇās.*

References

1. T.W. Rhys Davids and William Stede, *Pali English Dictionary* p. 203

2-3. *Ibid* p. 274

4. *Majjhima Nikāya*. Vol. I pp. 118-119 (Nalanda) "*Pañcme, bhikkhave, Kāmaguṇā*".

"*Iṭṭhā Kantā manāpā pīyarūpā kāmupasaṁhitā rajaniyā, sotaviññeyyā Saddhā.........*

I.B. Horner (trs.) *Middle Length Sayings* (translation of *Majjhima Nikāya*) Vol. I p. 112.

5. (i) *Kāma-taṇhā;* (ii) *bhava-taṇhā;* (iii) *Vibhava-taṇhā*

6. (i) *Kāmesanā;* (ii) *Bhavesanā;* (iii) *Brahmacariyesanā*

7. Four *upādāna* — *Kāma upādāna, diṭṭi-upādāna, selabbata - upādāna* and *attavāda - upādāna.*

8. Four *Āsavas* — *Kāmāsava, Bhavāsava, Diṭṭhi-āsava* and *Avejjā-āsava.*

9. Four *Ogha* — *Kāma-ogha, Bhava-ogha, Diṭṭhi-ogha* and *Avijjā-ogha.*

10. (i) *Kāmacchanda;* (ii) *Vyāpāda;* (iii) *Thīnamiddha;* (iv) *Uddhacca-kukucca;* (v) *Vicckicchā*

11. (i) *Kāmarāgai;* (ii) *Bhavarāga;* (iii) *Patigha*

(iv) *Māna;* (v) *Ditthi;* (vi) *Viccikicahā;* (vii) *Avijja.*

12. *Ten samyojanas* — *Sakkāyadiṭṭhi, Vicikicchā, Selabbataparāmāsa, Kāmarāga, Patigha, Rūpaāga, Arūparāga, Māna, Uddhacca, Avijjā.*

13. R. Morris (Ed) *Aṅguttara Nikāya* Vol. II p. 177.

14. *Pali English Dictionary* p. 203

15. T.W. Rhys Davids and J.E. Carpenter (Ed.) *Dīgha Nikāya* Vol. I. p. 71

16. T.W. Rhys Davids and J. E. Carpenter (Ed) *Sumaṅgala Vīlāsinī* (commentary on *Dīgha Nikāya*) Vol. I. P. 213

17. V. Treneker (Ed.) *Majjhima Nikāya* vol. I. p.364 Maurice Winternitz *History of Indian literature*. Vol. II. p. 72

18. R. Morris (Ed.) *Anguttara Nikāya* Vol. I p. 10 :

Pabhassaramidaṁ, bhikkhave, cittaṁ. Taṁ ca Kho āgantukehi upakkilesehi upakkiliṭṭhaṁ, ti pabhassaramidaṁ, bhikkhave, cittaṁ. Taṁ ca Kto āgantūkehi upakkileshei vippamutaṁ.

19. *Saṃyutta Nikāya* Vol. V.p.107. (Nalanda) F.L. Woodward (Trs.) *The Kindered Sayings* (translation of *Saṃyutta Nikāya)* p. 103.

20. T.W. Rhys Davids and J.E. Carpenter (Ed.) *Dīght Nikāya* Vol.II pp.290-315.

T.W. and C.A.F. Rhys Davids (Trs.) *Dialogues of the Buddha* (translation of *Dīgha Nikaya*). part-II pp. 322-346.

21. *Digha Nikāya* Vol. II p. 300

Dialogues of the Buddha. Part II pp. 334-335

22. J.L. Shastri (Ed.) *Ancient Indian Tradition and Mythology, Śiva-purāṇa : Śatarudra Saṁhita* Vol.II. Part II pp. 544-545.

XIII
Theory of Relation and Meditation in Buddhism

Bimalendra Kumar

It is seen that a hunter remains one pointed on a deer. After that there is the arising of a killing consciousness. Then, the natural question arises that what are those factors, which make a consciousness to kill a deer ? Again, a man intending to murder an enemy, has got to ponder over this act, its consequences etc. over and over again. A pleasurable interest and a joy arise in him at the thought of getting rid of this enemy and these in turn prompts him to continue his efforts and at last gathering up courage, he with his mind concentrated on the act of murder, would stab him or bring harm on him by some means. Here also a question arises that what are those factors of concentration which prompt him to do such acts ?

Again, great courage is necessary to give up the pleasures of the family life in order to embrace the life of an ascetic. A man never does so all of a sudden. Without pondering over the disadvantages and suffering of the worldly life, one cannot take to this new life of a religious medicant. After that, he desires for attaining spiritual perfection. Here, also the question arises that what are those factors by which a man gives up the worldly life, embraces the ascetic life and desires for spiritual perfection? Again, no moral deed such as charity can be performed by a feeble mind. Only after viewing attentively, considring fully the value of genorisity, one is able to give alms to the poor etc. Then, a question arises that what are those constituents by whose presence, one is able to sacrifice something to anyone ?

These questions generate an enquisitiveness and inspire to go deep down into the nature of reality to find out the suitable answers. But, the answers to these questions are very difficult. Here, coming to early Buddhist tradition and specially to the domain of *Abhidhammic* thought, there is the introduction of a theory of 'Realation', technically called as '*Paccaya*'. It is through the theory of 'Relation', the *Abhidhammic* thinkers have come forward in explaining these difficult problems.

'Relation' has been defined as that from which the fruit or effect derived from a cause comes - *paṭicca etasmā etīti paccàyo.*[1] It has the characteristic of rendering service.[2] The state, which renders service to the standing or arising of a state only, is said to be its cause or condition.[3] Thus, a relation (*paccaya*) is not only relating thing but also an assisting agency (*upakāraka*). A relation has four constituents. The one is which is related. The other is that to which one is relatted. The third one is the relation. The fourth one refers to those who donot come under such relation. The first one is technically called as *paccayadhamma*, the second one as *paccayupannadhamma*, the third one as *paccaya* and the last one as *paccanikadhamma*. There are twenty-four types of relations, which have been enumerated and illustrated in the *Paṭṭhānapakaraṇa*, the seventh and last book of the *Abhidhammapiṭaka*.[4] Among these twenty-four types of relations, *Jhāna-paccaya* (concentration relation) explains the problems related with meditation.

Tha Pāli word '*Jhāna*' (Skt. *dhyāna*) is tracted to two verbal forms. One is the verb '*jhāyati*, meaning to think or to meditate. The other derivation is traced to the verb *jhāpeti*, meaning 'to burn up'. It burns up opposing states, thus it is called as *Jhāna*. Ācārya Buddhaghosa says that *jhāna* has the characteristic mark of contemplation - "*ārammaṇaṁ upanjjhānato Paccanīka jhāpanato vā jhānaṁ.*

The word *Jhāna* is closely connected with another term '*Samādhi*', generally rendered as concentration. *Samādhi* derives from the prefixed verbal root *sam + ā + dhā,* meaning to collect or to bring together, thus suggesting the concentration or unification of the mind. Therefore, *samādhi* is briefly described as one-pointedness of wholesome *consciousness-Kusala-cittekaggatā Samādhi*[5].

It is evident from text that mind is *pure* (luminous) by its nature but obscured by incoming defiling elements.[6] These envelop the mind which loses its own natural state. it becomes fickle, restless and unsteady.[7] It wanders here and there and forms attachments to various types of sense data and indulges in sensual pleasure. The stonger in the amount of attachment, the greater is the degree of suffering.[8] Therefore, with the aim of removing the envelopment and bringing the mind back to its natural state, one proceeds to the practice of meditation.

First, one should know the cause of fickleness of the mind. It is said in this connection that there are five hindrances which make the mind restless. They are called *Nīvaraṇas*. They put obstacles in the way and dont allow the mind to concentrate on an object. They are *Kāmacchanda, vyāpāda, thīnamiddha, uddhacca-kukucca* and *vicikicchā*.[9] *Kāmacchanda* is the strong urge for sensual pleasure. *Vyāpāda* is ill-will or antipathy. It is a kind of desire to harm others. *Thīnamiddha* means sloth and torpar. Actually speaking, the laziness connected with mental states is *Thīna* and the same connected with consciousness is *Middha*. *Uddhacca-Kukucca* stands for restlessness and worry. In other words, it is the bewildering of the mind and brooding over what is done and what is not done. *Vicikicchā* is the term for doubt. In ordinary sense, it is a state of mind full of perplexity. Whereas in the technical sense, it is doubting the *Buddha, Dhamma* and *Saṅgha*.[10] So long as these hindrances are in force, it will be very difficult to obtain concentration of mind.

The disciple or aspirant to enlightenment, technically known as *yogāvacara*, endeavours to eradicate these hindrances, while their definitive eradication can only be achieved through the Insight (*vipassanā*) of Right understanding, their initial suppression is made possible with the arising of the *Jhānangas*, the constituents of *jhāna*-factors.[11]

In Generic sense, there are seven constituents of concentration (*jhānanga*). They are the *Vitakka, Vicāra Pīti, Somanassa, Domanassa, Upekkha* and *Ekaggatā*. With the help of these constituents, one gets concentration in moral consciousness and immoral consciousness.

In specific sense, there are five constituents only. They are the *Vitakka, vicāra, pīti, sukha* and *ekaggatā*. With the help of these, one gets *Rūpa-samādhi*. Here, the consciousness is always moral. *Vitakka* is the initial application of mind on the object-*ālambane cittassa abhiniropana lakkhano vitakko*'.[12] *Vicāra* is the sustaining of mind on the object- '*alambane cittasa anumajjana lakkhano vicāro*'.[13] *Pīti* is the thrill of pleasant sensation - '*Pīnayati tī pīti*'.[14] *Sukha* is the composure. It is saturation of joy within mind and body-*nāma rūpa abhibyāpanaṃ sukhaṃ*.[15] *Ekaggatā* is one pointedness - '*cittasa ekodibhāvo*.[16]

Thus, with each *jhāna*-factor, having a definite function to fulfil, the hindrances are suppressed and become functionless. Following which, there arise the five constituents of *jhāna*, Technically called *Jhānangas*. It should be understood that all the *jhāna*-factors donot suppress all the hindrances : One pointedness (*ekaggatā*) suppresses sensual pleasure ; pleasant sensation (*pīti*) weakens ill-will; the application of mind (*vitakka*) makes sloth and torpor dormant ; composure (*sukha*) suppresses restlessness and worry (*uddhaccakukucca*); and sustained application of mind (*vicāra*) curtails the activities of sceptical doubt. In this manner, the hindrances are suppressed and the *jhāna*-factors. begin to function. Against this background, the meditator endeavours to attain concentration.

Each *jhāna* factor has to do something after they arise.[17] The first factor helps a man to draw his restless mind from different directions and directs it towards the object. The second one keeps it on the object. The third generates hopes of realization of the desire. The fourth one functions in developing composure both in mind and body and makes them saturated with it. The last one prepares then a congenial atmosphere for generation of one-pointedness.[18] In this way, with the appearance and functioning of the *jhāna* factors, there becomes the possibility of suppression of the hindrances for which also there is a process.[19]

The five stages of *Jhāna* gradually appear and the consciousness gets concentration. The five strages are namely *paṭhama-jhāna, dutiya-jhāna, tatiya-jhāna, catuttha-jhāna* and *pañcama-jhāna.*

In the first stage, all the five *jhāna* factors are at work and therby concentration is achieved. It is called first stage of *rūpa-jhāna*. Gradually, the mind is trained and therefore, there is no need of initially applying the mind on all objects. Therefore, the *vitakka* becomes absent. A further stage of *jhāna* is attained with four *jhāna* factors namely, *vicāra, pīti, sukha* and *ekaggatā.*

Further, the mind is trained and there is no need of generation of thrill of pleasant sensation. Therefore, *pīti* becomes also absent. There remain two *jhāna* factors namely, *sukha* and *ekaggatā* and with them, a stage of *jhāna* is obtained and it is called the fourth stage of *Rūpa-jhāna.*

The mind further receives training. The recluse now feels pleasure in meditating on the object. Therefore, he is cautious about the fact that he may get attached with the object itself and in this way, the *sukha* is replaced by *upekkhā*.

We see that in the presence of *jhāna* - factors, there are five stages of *Jhānaṅgas*, namely *paṭhama-Jhāna, Dutiya Jhāna*...etc. In this way, there are in one side the *Jhāna*-factors and on the other side, there are the consciousness associated with that. This is done by a relation known as *Jhāna-paccaya*. Therefore, the *Jhāna-paccaya* is a type of relation, in which the *paccayadhamma* may be one of the *Jhānaṅgas* and the *paccayuppannadhamma* may be consciousness, arising with that. It may be understood in term of *Jhāna*-factor and the *Paṭhama-jhāna* factor. The five constituents in this case are the *paccayadhamma* and the first *Rūpa-jhāna* consciousness is the *paccayuppannadhamma*. Similarly, *upekkhā* and *ekaggatā* serve as *paccayadhamma* in arising of the first *Arūpajjhāna* consciousness. The *Paṭṭhāna-pakaraṇa* states - '*jhānaṅgāni jhāna sampayuttakānaṃ taṃ samuṭṭhānaṃ ca rūpānaṃ jhānapaccayena paccayo*.[20]

In this relation, *paccayadhammas* are the seven constituents of *Jhāna*, namely *vitakka, vicāra, pīti, ekaggatā, somanassa domanassa* and *upekkhā*. And the *paccayuppannadhammas* are all the types of consciousness, with the exception of twice fold *viññāṇa*, their concomitants, and the material qualities in co-existence with the seven constituents.[21]

The factor of *ekaggatā* in the sense of 'attention' is common to all forms of consciousness and as such *ekaggatā* as a property of the meditative mind, is to be understood as 'sustained attention' or 'concentration' as distinguished from the former. The three factors of *somanassa, domanassa* and *upekkhā*, being but the different forms of *vedanā* (feeling) are sometimes referred to by the single term '*vedanā*'. Now, *vedanā* like *ekaggatā* is also a common property of all forms of consciousness.[22] The factor of *domanassa*, which is absolutely immoral, can be found only in the two forms of immoral consciousness rooted in hatred (*paṭigha*).[23] The other six factors can be found only in all classes of consciousness—moral, immoral or non-moral.

Thus, without the influence of constituents of *Jhāna*,. we should not be able to observe any distinctions in forms. Without it, we should not be able to make or take even a single right step. A man may aim eastward, but he will swere southward and fall westward. During this wavering step, his mind may wander from one object to another object and become forgetful of the first. In such a state of mental distraction, he would not be able to repeat even the easiest lesson.

Lastly, the factors of contemplation *(jhānaṅga)* serve the religious life by way of *Jhāna-paccaya*, as a result of which one is able to develop the highter contemplations and thus attin spiritual perfection by the culture of the mind. On the way to *Nibbāna*, recluse serves to promote spiritual development to diminish, the impact of suffering to calm the mind and to reveal the true facts of existence. This *Nibbāna*, the ultimate goal, can be achieved through the practice of *Vipassanā* meditation. *Passanā* is a Pali ward, meaning to see with open eyes. *Vipassanā* means to see in a special way, i.e. to observe things as they really are, not just as they appear to be. In other words, *vipassanā* is a technique of self observation and the ultivation of such potentialities to perfection and the developement of the precepts. The technique is also known as the meditation of mindfulness or awareness of insight.

Vipassanā begins as the observation of respiration, through that of the body and its different view-points and the bodily sensations or feelings and mental disposition to that of *dhammas* such as impermanance, momentary *flux*, *Anatta* and *Dukkha*. This practice is conducted through observation alone without the interference of *vitakka* and *vicāra*.

Therefoer, a practisenor starts the practice, first of all, by observaing respiration — the flow of incoming breath and outgoing breath. Two things happen at this stage of the practice ; gradually the mind gets concentrated on the process of respiration and the practisenor becomes aware of the relationship between mental states and respiration. It will be observed that whenever there is some agitation in the mind due to anger hatred, fear, passion - the normal respiration is affected ; it gets disturbed. Although this happens all the time, the student discovers it for the first time - a big discovery indeed. He continues the practice unruffled by the change in respiration. As the mind gets more and more concentrated, the practisenor advances on the path of development of mental absorption - *jhānic* state and can be progressively led on the path of eight *jhānas-absorption* - the region of *samādhi.*

The Buddha is not content with the absorption stage. The aim to achieve total purification of the mind and *Ānāpāna* is taken as a means to reach the higher goal of eradication of defilements from the deepest level of the unconscious mind.

Thus, *vipassana* meditation should be practised by one and all in the strife-torn world of today. By contemplating the object for *vipassanā*, one can get rid of suffering of ribirth, old age, disease and death. Moreover, the person practising meditation can attain the supreme state of emancipation called *Nibbāna*.

Reference

1. Dwarka Das Shastri (Ed.) *Visuddhimagga* p. 450
2. *'upakārako lakkhano paccayo'- Idem.*
3. *'yo hi dhammo yassa dhammassa thitiyā vā upattiyā vā upakārako hoti, tassa paccayo ti vuccati - Idem.*
4. *Paṭṭhāna* Vol. I, pp. 3-11.
5. Dwarka Das Shastri op-cit p. 84
6. *Anguttgra Nikāya* Vol.I p. 10 (Nalanda)
7. *Dhammapada Gatha* : 33
8. Udāna p.92 *'Yesaṃ sataṃ piyāni, sataṃ tesaṃ dukkhāni------yesaṃ ekaṃ piyaṃ ekaṃ tesaṃ dukkhaṃ.*
9. P.V. Bapat and R.D. Vadekar (Ed) *Dhamma Saṁgani* pp. 204-205
10. *Idem*
11. Digha Nikāya *'Yathā iṇam, yathā rogaṃ, yathā bandhanāgāraṃ, yathā dāsabyaṃ yathā kantāraddhānamaggaṃ, evaṃ ime pañca nīvarane appatine attani samanupsati. yathā ānanyaṃ, yathā ārogyaṃ, yathā bandhanā mokkhaṃ, yathā khemantabhūnim, evaṃ eva, ime pañca nīvaraṇe pahīne attani samanupassati'- Vol. I p. 73 (Nalanda)*
12. P.V. Bapat and R.D. Vadekar *Aṭṭhasālini* p. 75
13. *Ibid.*, p. 95; Dwarka Das Shastri (Ed.) *Milindapañhāpali* p. 75

14. *Idem*

15. *Ibid.*, p.96

16. *Ibid.*, p. 97

17. *Dīgha Nikāya* Vol. I pp. 65-66 (Nalanda) ; *Dhamma Saṅgani* pp. 45-70

18. Bhadanta Revatadhamma (Ed.) Abhidhammattha *Sangaho* I pp. 94-96

19. *Dīgha Nikāya* Vol. I pp. 45-70, 65-66 (Nalanda)

20. *Paṭṭhāna* Vol. I p.9 (Nalanda) ; *Paṭṭhāna Aṭṭhākatha* (Nalanda), p. 78

21. Paṭṭhāna Aṭṭhakatha (Nalanda) "*Upanijjhāyanaṭṭhe-naupakārakāni ṭhapetvā dvipañ- caviññāṇesu kāyika-sukhadukkhavedanādyayaṃ sabbāni pi kusalādibhedāni satta jhānaṅgāni jhāna-paccayo-* p.78.

22. Bradanta Revatadhamma op.- cit. I. *Phasso, vedanā, saññā, cetanā, ekaggatā, jīvitindriyaṃ manasikāro ceti sattime cetasikāsa bbacittasādhāraṇā nāma* - p. 99

23. Ibid., p. 37. *Domanass asahagataṃ paṭighasampayuttaṃ asaṅkhārikamekaṃ, sasaṅkhāri kame kaṃ ti imāni dve pi paṭighasampayuttacittāni nāma.*

XIV
Vipassanā and Relation with Puggala-paññatti

Om Prakash Pathak

Vipassanā is a very ancient meditation technique of India, rediscovered about 2500 years ago by Lord Buddha, the Enlightended One. The technique helped a large section of the people of India to come out of their suffering and attain a high level of growth in all spheres of human activity. The practice of *Vipassanā* brings about a real transformation in human personality and attitude.

The word '*Vipassanā*' has two component parts - '*Vī*' and '*passanā*! '*Vī*' is the prefix which means 'revealing' and '*passanā*' means 'seeing, observing, inward vision, insight, intuition etc,. It means to see things as they are, to see things in their true perspective, in their true nature. It is, in essence, a technique of self observation, true observation, self exploration.

The questions that arise in this context are : *why vipassanā a meditation* ? The human being is a rational animal. He always wants to think, to know and understand all things. From time to time he wonders, *why am I born? What is the purpose of life ? What is this whole universe about* ? Most often these questions lead him only into confusion and more uncertainty. But the Lord Buddha has clearly stated that *Vipassanā* is the only way for making the mind pure destroying all kind of suffering visualizing the higher truth and realizing *Nibbāna* face to face. The Buddha is very much emphatic in this :

"Ekāyano ayaṁ, bhikkhave, maggo sattānaṁ

visuddhiyā, sokaparidevānaṁ samatikkamāya,

dukkha domanassānaṁ atthaṁ gamāya,

ñāyassa adhigamāya nibbānassa

sacchikiriyāya yadidaṁcattāro satipaṭṭhānā".[1]

It means that this is the only way, O monks, for the purification of beings, for the overcoming of sorrow and misery, for the destruction of pain and grief, for gaining the knowledge, for attainmpnt of *Nibbāna,* the arousing of four mindfulness (*Satipaṭṭhāna*).

The word *Satipaṭṭhāna* (mindfulness) has two componet parts : *Sati* and *Paṭṭhāna. 'Sati'* means mindfulness and '*Paṭṭhāna*' denotes the sense of presence. It means that the presence of mindfulness is *Satipaṭṭhāna.* Here the term *Satipaṭṭhāna* may be broken as *Sati* and *Upaṭṭhāna*' expresses the sense of arousing, making alert and functioning etc. Again the term *Paṭṭāna* means a sound base for making right efforts for gradually removing the layers of pollutions and realizeation of a state of Eternal Bliss, i.e. *Nibbāna.* In this sense, *Satipaṭṭhāna* is the light of awareness which serves as a base for moral efforts for purificational gain.[2]

Lord Buddha has referred to Vipassanā in following words:

"I dha āyuso Sāriputta, bhikkhu paṭisalliānārāmo

hoti, paṭisallamarato, ajjhattaṁ cetosamath

amanuyuttho anirākatajjhāno Vipassanāya

samannāgato".[3]

It means, here, Reverend Sariputta, monk delights in solitary meditation, he delighted by solitary meditation, he is intent on mental tranquillity within, his meditation is uninterrupted, he is endowed with vision, a cultivator of empty places.

In this context, *Vipassanā* or *meditation* or *Satipaṭṭhāna* is briefly described as the presence of Awareness. It is fourfold practice to purify the mind as - *Kāyānupassanā, Vedanānupassanā, Cittānupassanā and Dhammānupassanā.* It has been stated as four, not more than this and not less with full consideration of the benefits of the men to be led towards the state of *Nibbāna*. The *Kāyānupassanā* and *Vedanānupassanā* are the paths for the persons with dominence of attachment and engaged in getting purification through the *Samatha*. Further, the *Cittānpassanā* and *Dhammānupassanā* are the paths for the persons who are desirous of getting purification through *Vipassanā*. The functions of *Samatha* and *Vipassanā* are clearly mentioned in the text :

"Monks, these two conditions lead to knowledge. What two ? *Samatha* and *Vipassanā*. if cultivated, what benefit does *Smatha* confer ? The mind is cultivated. What benefit does result from a cultivated mind ? All lust is abandoned. Monks, if *Vipassanā* is to be cultivated, what benefit does it confer ? Insight is cultivated. If insight be cultivated, what benefit does it confer ? All ignorance is abandoned. A mind defiled by lust, monks, is not set free; nor can insight defiled by ignorance be cultivated. Indeed, monks, the freedom from lust leads to release of the tranquillity of mind, the freedom from ignorance leads to the release of the insight".[4]

The purpose of *Samatha* is to induce concentration in the mind and free it from all distraction. The essence of *Vipassanā* is to see the truth as it is. The two jointly act as a single harmonious entity as the way to *Nibbāna*.[5]

Now question arises how it is practised ? First of all, a man, selects the object of *meditation* or *Vipassanā,* then selects a place for practice of the *Vipassanā*. The texts has mentioned that the suitable places for the purpose of *Vipassanā* are the secluded dwellings, a forest, the foot of a tree, a mountain, an open sky and the heap of straw.[6] The later text, *Visuddhimagga* also mentions that the five places are suitable for *Vipassanā*. It should be neither too far from the village nor too near. It should be little frequented in the day and remain tranquil in the night. There should be no external disturbances such as from creeping creatures, serpents and so on. It should be inhabited by the learned monks.[7]

After taking the object and selecting a suitable place, the person sits in a cross legged posture, keeping the body erect and the mindfulness awakened around his face. he is at that time quite ardent, conscious and mindful with total destruction of greed and hatred towards the beings of the universe and prepares a soothing mental atmosphere for complete awareness of his own beings within and without. It is natural that in the background of the contanct, both internal and external, sensations arise. He on that occasion remains conscious and a detached onlooker towards them. Whatever type of sensations may arise, he is aware of them. The greater is the number of attachment, the bigger is the number os suffering. The Buddha says :

> *"Yassa sahassaṁ piyāmdukkhaṁ pi sahassaṁ,*
>
> *yassa sataṁ piyaṁ dukkhaṁ pi sataṁ,*
>
> *yassa ekaṁ piyaṁ dukkhaṁ pi ekaṁ,*
>
> *yassa natthi piyaṁ dukkhaṁ pi natthi".*[8]

It means that if one has thousand attachments, thousand fold is suffering, if one has hundred attachments, suffering is hundred fold, if single attachment, suffering is also one and when there is no attachment there is no suffering at all.

In this context, *Puggala-Paññatti* presents a brief description of the persons who are engrossed in *Meditation* or *Insight or Vipassanā*. And total number of the persons are three hundred and ninty, but out of them, only some persons are engrossed in *Meditation or Vipassanā*. Who are they? They are :

1. *Cętosamathassa Lābhī Puggala*[9]
2. *Adhipaññādhammavipassanāya Lābhī Puggala*[10]
3. *Kuppadhamma Puggala*[11]
4. *Parihānadhamma Puggala*[12]
5. *Cetanābhabba Puggala*[13]
6. *Anurakkhaṇābhabba Puggala*[14] etc.

These types of *Puggala* (person) are engrossed in *Vipassanā Meditation* in the stage of *Rūpa Jhāna, Arūpa Jhāna* and *Lokuttara Jhāna*. Here, I am describing each of *Vipassi Puggala* (meditator person).

1. *Cetosamathassa Lābhī Puggala :*

The word '*Cetosamatha*' has two component parts - *Çeto* and *Samatha*. '*Ceto*' means mind and '*Samatha*' means 'tranquillity, calm, peace' etc. It means tranquillity, calm, peace' etc. It means tranquillity of mind.

'*Lābhī*' means attainer. It means those who have attained the tranquillity of mind. He attains the tranquillity of mind by eight *Samāpatti*,[15] i.e. four *Rūpa Jhāna* and four *Arūpa Jhāna*. Here *Rūpa* means an object associated with form and colour. It is generally gross in nature. Concentration obtained on such object is, technically, called *Rūpa-Jhāna*. The term *Arūpa* refers to such type of object which is formless. It has neither shape nor colour. It is completely formless and subtle in its nature. Concentration of mind obtained on such an object is called *Arūpa-Jhāna*.

There are four stages of *Rūpa-Jhāna*, i.e. *Paṭhama-Jhāna, Dutiya-Jhāna, Tatiya-Jhāna* and *Catuttha-Jhāna*. In the first stage of *Rūpa-Jhāna*, all the *Jhānic* factors, *Vitakka, Vicāra, Pītī, Sukha* and *Ekaggatā* remain present. Functioning individually and also in association, they generate an atmosphere of one-pointedness of the consciousness. The attainment of concentration with their association is called *Paṭhama-Rūpa-Jhāna*. After continous practice, the mind is little relieved of its flickering nature. It, by itself, tends towards the object, the initial application is not needed. As such, in the second stage of *Rūpa-Jhāna*, the first two *Jhāna*-factors e.g. *Vitakka* and *Vicāra* become extinct. It is attained with the remaining three *Jhāna*-factor, i.e. *Pīti, Sukha* and *Ekaggatā*. Further, in the backgraound of *Jhānic* maturity, the *Pīti* also becomes extinct in the third stage of *Rūpa-Jhāna*. It is attained with remaining two Jhāna-factors e.g. *Sukha* and *Ekaggatā* only. In the process of his gradual *Jhānic* maturity the *Yogāvacara* starts experiencing serenity within and without. The external wandering of the consciousness is gradually curtailed. Again, so that it may not develop attachment with the object of meditation itself, the fourth *jhānic*-factor *Sukha* is replaced by *Upekkhā*. Thus the fourth stage of *Rūpa-Jhāna* is attained with two *Jhānic* factors, *upekkhā* and *Ekaggatā*. In this way, with such *Rūpa-Samādhi* or *Rūpa-Jhāna*, the consciousness of the *Yogāvacara* becomes pure, free from defilements, mild, pliable, steady and concentrated.

Again, he proceeds up to a formless object and exherts for *Arūpa-Jhāna* for making his consciousness more subtle. While practising the *Rūpa-Jhāna* the *Yogāvacara* has before him an object associated with form. He has attained mastery over it and reduces or extends it as he likes. In the last phase, he develops it so as to pervade everywhere. Wherever he sees, there is that object. Then with a view to go for the *Arūpa-Jhāna*, he with his meditational power removes it and finds before him the infinite space (*Ananta Ākāsa*). He takes this infinite-space as the object of his *Jhāna* and makes right efforts for developing concentration. In due course, there comes a moment when he attains concentration on such a formless object. This achievement is called the first stage of *Arūpa-Jhāna*, technically called *Ākāsānañcāyatana*. In course of his gradual maturity of concentration, he comes to understand that the infinite space is nothing but the manifestation of his consciousness. It is his consciousness which is pervading all over as an infinite space. With this, he gives up the previous object and takes infinite consciousness (*Ananta viññāṇa*) as the object of his *Jhāna*. During the course of his right efforts, there comes a moment, when he gets concentration on it. It is the second stage of *Arūpa-Jhāna*, technically known as *Viññāṇañcāyatana*. The gradual achievement in his *Jhānic* persuit, encourages him to go higher and higher. Now he mentally analyses the nature of infinite consciousness and realizes that it is also nothing, empty of anything. This nothingness of consciousness then becomes his object and he develops *Jhāna* on its. Attainment of concentration on it is the third stage of *Arūpa-Jhāna*, technically known as *Ākiñcaññāyatana*. He further goes on meditation on the same object and in this process there comes a moment when his mind becomes immensely subtle. It loses the discrimination of subject and object. Its functions come to a stop and it is established in itself. There is consciousness, but there is no functioning of it. Achievement of this stage is the fourth stage of *Arūpa-Jhāna*, technically known as *Nevasaññānāsaññāyatana*. In this meditation process, the mind becomes immensely pure tranquilised and free from all defiling factors.

2. *Adhipaññādhammavipassanāya*[19] *Lābhī puggala :*

It means that those persons who have attained the higher wisdom of insight (*vipassanā*) into things, have already attained the inner tranquillity of mind. Therefore, the *Aṭṭhakathā* says that this type of person is known as *Sukhavipassaka-Ariyasāvaka Puggala.*[17] It is the stage of *Lokuttara* or Supramundane. Like *Rūpa Samādhi,* in this stage, there are forty types of Supramundane consciousness or forty types of *Jhāna* factors for meditation. But this stage is higher than the *Rūpa Samādhi*. There are forty stages of *Lokuttara Jhāna*. Each of them is called a stage of *Jhāna*, and in this way there are forty stages of *Jhāna* as *Paṭhama-Jhāna Dutiya-Jhāna, Tatiya-Jhāna, Catuttha-Jhāna* and *Pañcama-Jhāna* in *Sotāpatti Magga* and *Phala, Sakadāgāmī Magga* and *Phala, Anāgāmī-Magga* and *Phala, Arhata Magga* and *Phala*. Each of them containing five *Jhāna*. In this way, the *yogāvacara* attains the *Jhāna* meditation, then he eliminates ten fetters, i.e. *Sakkāyadiṭṭhi*

(Self-illusion), *Vicikicchā* (doubts), *Silabbataparāmāsa* (Adherence to wrongful rites and ceremonies), *Kāma-rāga* (sensuous desire), *Paṭigha* (ill-will), *Rūpa-Rāga* (attachment for Rūpa existence), *Arūpa-Rāga* (attachment for Arūpa existence), *Māna* (conceit), *Uddhacca* (Restlessness), and *Avijjā* (Ignorance). On his path of meditation, during the *sotāpatti* stage, he eliminates the first three fetters. He weakens the next two fetters in the stage of *Sakadāgāmī*. In the *Anāgāmī* stage, weakens fetters eliminates the last five fetters eliminates in the stage of *Arhata*. In this way, his mind becomes pure, pliable, concentrated and immensely subtle. With this subtle *Jhānic meditation*, he attains the final goal of life, i.e. *Nibbāna*, a state of eternal bliss.

> "*Padamaccuta maccantaṁ, Asaṅkhataṁ anuttaraṁ, Nibbānamiti bhāsanti, Vānamuttā mahesayo.*"[18]

3. *Kuppadhamma Puggala :*

Kuppadhamma means perturbable nature or liable to perturbation or one who has not yet attained full mastery over the mind. It is applied to an ordinary person who has attained *eight Samāpattis*, i.e. four *Rūpa-Jhāna* and four *Arūpa-Jhāna*. It is also applied to a stream-attainer (*Sotāpanna*) and to a once-returner (*Sakadāgāmī*). It means a person who is unsteady or not firmly established in the path. It is so called because in his case, the mental conditions which are antagonistic to *Samādhi* and *Vipassanā* have not been completely stopped nor well-washed off, and it is for this reason that their attainment perishes and falls away.[19] The text, *Puggala-Paññatti* deals with *Akuppadhamma Puggala*.[20] It is applied to an Never-returner (*Anāgāmī*) who has attained eight *Samāpattis* and also to a *Khīṇāsava*, i.e. a person who has destroyed passions. It means a person who does not go astray. He is steady or firmly established in the path. Hindrances to *Samādhi* and *Vipassanā* in such a person are completely destroyed. His attainment is not destroyed by useless talks, or by any other unsuitable act committed through negligence.[21]

4. *Parihānadhamma - Puggala* :

It means liable to decline or fall away. Someone reaches to attainment of the *Rūpa-Jhāna* and *Arūpa-Jhāna.* But he does not reach them according to his wish, and not without trouble and exhertion; it is not according to his wish with regard to place, object and duration, that does he enter them, or rise therefrom. Therefore it is well possible that such a person, through negligence may lose these attainments. Such a person is said to be liable to decline or fall away.[22] The text, *Aṅguttara-Nikāya* says that this type of person is associated with *Kammārāmatā, Bhassārāmatā* and *Niddārāmatā*[23] because they do bad actions and false speech. *Aṭṭhakathā* says that the *Kuppadhamma, Akuppadhamma, Parihānadhamma* and *Aparihānadhamma puggala* are the same categories, only name is differnt. These types of *puggala* can obtain the *Vipassanā* meditation but they may fall or may not fall.

5. *Cetanābhabba Puggala* :

'*Cetanā*' means will, volition, intention, purpose etc. and 'Bhabba' means able, capable, competent etc.[24] It means, a person, who is competent in will. Here a person obtains the *Vipassanā Meditation* by *eight Samāpattis* (attainments). When he desires and as long as he follows this up by willing, then he does not fall away from those attainments. But if he does not so will, he does fall away from them.[25] Therefore such a person is called one who is competent in will.

6. *Anurakkhaṇābhabba Puggala* :

Anurakkhaṇābhabba has two component parts - *Anurakkhaṇā* and *bhabba.* '*Anurakkhaṇā*' means watchfulness and '*bhabba*' means competent, capable etc. It means, a person, who is competent in watchfulness. If he obtains the *Vipassana* Medition by *eight Samāpattis*, then he does not fall away from them if he is watchful or is not watchful. In both ways he can meditate without any hindrances. *Aṭṭhakathā* says that competent person (*bhabba puggala*) is of two types, that is *Cetanābhabba* and *Anurakkhaṇābhabbas Puggala.*[26] *Cetanābhabba Puggala* does not know that what is the acceptable feeling and what is not ? But *Anurakkhaṇābhabba Puggala* knows each and every thing.

In this way the practice of *Vipassanā* brings a real transformation of the human personality and with such a practice, the consciousness of the *Yogāvacara* becomes pure and free from all defilements and he attains the final goal of life.

References :

1. *Dāgha Nikāya* , Vol. II, p. 217. (Nalanda)

2. *Sumaṅgalavilāsini* Vol. III pp. 63-66.(Nalanda)

3. *Majjhima Nikāya,* Vol. I, p. 264.(Nalanda)

4. *Aṅguttara Nikāya*, Vol I, p. 58. (Nalanda)

5. *Paṭisambhidāmagga*, p. 25. (Nalanda)

6. *Majjhima Nikāya*, Vol. I, p. 61. (Nalanda)

7. D. D. Kosambi (Ed.) *Visuddhimagga* p. 95.

8. *Khuddak Nikāya* p. 175. (Nalanda)

9. *Puggala-Paññatti*, pp. 91-94. (Nalanda)

10. *Ibid.* pp.91-94.

11. *Ibid* p. 19.

12. *Ibid.*, p. 20.

13. *Idem.*

14. *Ibid.* pp. 20-21.

15. Ibid p. 91 "*Idhekacco puggalo lābhí hoti rūpasahagatāṇaṁ vā arūpasaahagatānaṁ vā samāpattinaṁ na lābhi lokuttara maggassa vā phalassa vā*".

16. Dwarakadass, Shastri, "*Ārammanaṁ ca patisaṅkā bhaṅgaṁ ca anupassati, suññato' ca upaṭṭhānaṁ adhipaññā Vipassanā ti*". "*Sā adhipaññā ca dhammesu ca vipassanā" ti kativā adhipaññā-dhammavipassanā ti vuccati, tāya niccasārābhāvassa*

ca attasārābhāvassa ca sutthu ditthatā sārādānābhinivesassa pahānam hoti.

Visuddhimagga, p. 586.

17. Mahesh Tiwary, *Ppuggala-paññatti-Atthakathā*, p.117.(Nalanda)

18. D. D. Kosambi *Abhidhammatthasṅgho* p. 125.

19. B.C. Law (Tr.) *Designation of Human Types*, p. 4.

20. *Pugala-paññatti*, p. 19.

21. Mahesh Tiwary, (Ed) *Pañcappakaraṁa Aṭṭhakathā*, Vol. I, p. 47.

22. *Puggala* - paññatti, p. 20.

23. *Aṅguttara Nikāya* Vol, III, p. 29. (Nalanda)

24. *Pañcappakaraṇs Atthakathā*, Vol. I, p. 47.*"Cetanābhabbo ti cetanāya aparihāniṁ āpajjituṁ bhabbo"*.

25. *Puggala Paññatti.* p.20. (Nalanda).

26. *Panñcappakaraṇs Aṭṭhakathā, Vol. I, p. 48. "I me dve pi samāpatiṁ thapetuṁ thāvaraṁ kātuṁ paṭibalā. Cetanābhabbato pana anurakkhanābhabbo balavataro. Cetanābhabbo hi upak ārānupak āradhamme na jānāti Anurakbhanbbo upakārānupakāradhamme jānāti"*.

XV

Vippassanā and Aśoka's Dhamma

D.C. Ahir

The name and fame of Asoka, the great Emperor of India, is well-known throughout the whole world. Paying tribute to him H.G.Wells, the great historian of modern times, says: "Amidst the tens of thousands of names of monarchs that crowd the columns of history, their majesties and graciousnesses and serenities and royal highnessess and the like, the name of Aśoka shines, and shines almost alone, a star".[1]

Aśoka was the grandon of Chandragupta, the founder of the Maurya dynasty. After the death of his father, Bindusara, Aśoka ascended the Magadha throne in 273 B.C. His coronation, however, took place in 269 B.C.

Aśoka was fortunate in inheriting a well-established Empire which included almost the whole of modern India, excepting Orissa and the far south, Pakistan and Afghanistan. To this vast empire, Asoka added Kalinga (modern Orissa), which he conquesred after a bloody war. The large-scale massacre in the Kalinga war deeply influenced his mind and brought revolution in his character. With this event, his outlook, both in his pesrsonal and public life, changed. Consequently, he was drawn to the mild teachings of the Compassionate Buddha. After adopting the Buddha's teachings. he desclared that henceforth he would prefer '*Dhamma-vijaya*' to '*Rājya-Vijaya*'. In other words, he took a vow to win the hearts of the people, both inside and outside the borders of his Empire, by pesrsuasion and love, instead of by the use of force and sword.

Aśoka speaks to us through his inscriptions on the rocks and pillars which have since been discovered at 40 places in India, (34), Nepal, (2) Pakistan, (2) and Afghanistan (2). All the inscriptions found in India and Nepal are composed in various forms of Prākrit and are written in the Brāhmi script. The two inscriptions at Shahbazgarhi and Manseshra in Pakistan are written in Kharoshṭhi. An inscription discovered at Kandhar in Afghanistan is bi-lingulal, in Greek and Aramaic. In all the reçords, Asoka refers to himself as *'Devānāmpiyapiyadasi Rājā (the Beloved of the Gods, the king Piyadasi).* Only in two versions of Minor[2] Rock Edict I, the king's name is mesntioned.

In his edicts, Aśoka time and again refers to *'Dhamma'* and exhorts one and all to inculcate the practice of *Dhamma.* What was meant by *'Dhamma'* by Aśoka has been a subject of comment by the historians. Some scholars have even opined that *Aśoka's dhamma* was his own innovation and it had nothing to do with the *'Buddha-Dhamma'.* This is not a correct interpretation. Asoka propagated *Dhamma* as taught by the Buddha. This is very well confirmed by the evidence that Asoka himself provides in his edicts.

In one of the earliest rock edicts to be issued by Asoka, he says:[3]

> "A little more than two years and a half passesd since I am avowedly a lay follwer of the Buddha. But I was not vigorously exerting myself in the cause of *Dhamma* for the first one year. However,it is little more than a year that I am devotedly attached to the *Saṅgha* and exerting myslef vigorously".

The above edict, now known as Minor Rock Edict I has been discovered at as many as 14 places in India. This means that Asoka gave widest publicity to his increasing devotion to the Buddha's teachings.

In the third Minor Rock Edict, which has been discovered only at Bairat near Jaipur, Rajasthan, Asoka says:[4]

> "King Piyadasi of Magadha salutes the monks of the *Saṅgha*, wishes them good health and comfort in their movement, and addresses them in the following words. It is known to you, Venerable Sirs, how far extends my reverence for and faith in the Buddha, the *Dhamma* and the *Saṅgha*. Whatever, Venerable Sirs,has been said by the Lord Buddha, all that is well-said. But Venerable Sirs, I deem it proper to speak out what appears to me the way a to how the true *Dhamma* may be of long duration",

Asoka then goes on to list seven texts[5] of *Dhamma* (for details please see note 5), and directs that the monks and nuns may constantly listen to and remember these texts. Likewise lay men and lay women too.

Asoka not only suggested constant study of certain texts by the monks, nuns and the laity, he also took keen interst in the affairs of the *saṅgha*. He even endeavoured to check schism in the *Saṅgha*. In the Miner Pillar Edict I found at Allahabad-Kosam, Sanchi and Sarnath, Asoka addresses the monks and nuns in these words:[6]

> "No one is to cause dissension in the Order. Whoever creates a schism in the Order, whether monk or nun is to be dressed in white garments, and to be put in a place not inhabited by monks or nuns. For it is my wish that the Order should remain united and endure for long".

Asoka's own words, quoted above make it clear that he was a devout follower of the Buddha. Not only he refers to the Buddha, the *Dhamma* and the *Saṅgha*, the Buddha is also represented in the edicts by the well-knowns symbol of the white elephant[7] which is indicated by an inscription at Girnar at the end of R.E. XIII, and representd by a figure cut on the rock at Dhauli, and incised at Kalsi with the label '*gajatame*', "the most perfect elephant". The elelphant stands for the Buddha's descent on earth as His mother saw in dream, before conception, a white elephant entering her womb. The four anmials toping the Asoka pillars are: the Elephant, the Bull, the Horse and the Lion. These animals were chosen by Asoka as they are associated with the Buddha. The Elephant typifies, Conception, the Bull indicates Nativity, Buddha's birth as a human being, the Horse stands for the Buddha's Renunciation, and the Lion represents Buddha as the great Teacher. Four Lions facing four directions indicate that the Buddha (*Sâkya-simha*) preached in all the directions and to all the mankind.

Asoka 's devotion to the Buddha is evident from some other facts also, such as, his pilgrimage to the holy shrines; his observance of *uposatha;* Asoka nowhere in his edicts calls it '*Buddha-Dhamma*'. He merely calls it '*Dhamma*' or '*Dharma*' everywhere. The essence of *Dhamma* has been elucidated by Asoka in five principal edicts, viz., three rock edicts and two pillar edicts.

In the third Major Rock Edict found at Girnar in Gujarat, Asoka defines *Dhamma* in these words :

> **"It is good to be obedient to one's mother and father, friends and relatives, to be generous to *brāhmaṇa* and *śramaṇas*, it is good not to kill living beings, it is good not only spend little, but to own the minimum of property"[8].**

In the fourth Major Rock Edict, at Girnar, Asoka says:[9]

> **"Through his (Asoka's) instruction in *Dhamma*, abstention from killing and non-injury to living beings,deference to relatives, *brāhmaṇas* and *śramaṇas*, obedience to mother and father, and obedience to elders have all increased as never before for centuries".**

Again in the Major Rock Edit No. XI found at Kalsi, near Dehradun it Uttar Pradesh, Asoka says :[10]

> "There is no gift comparable to the gift of *Dhamma*, the praise o *Dhamma*, the sharing of *Dhamma*, fellowship in *Dhamma*. And this is good behaviour towards friends,acquaintances and relatives and towards *śramaṇas* and *brāhmaṇas*, and abstention from killing living beings".

Of the seven Major Pillar Edicts, *Dhamma* is specifically defined in two edicts. In edict No. II, on the Topra Pillar now standing at Ferozshah Kotla, Delhi, Asoka says:[11]

> "The practices of *Dhamma* are meritorious. But what does *Dhamma* consist of ? It consists of the least amount of sin,many virtuous deeds, compssion, liberality, truthfulness and purity".

Again in edict No. VII on the same Delhi-Topra pillar, Asoka says:[12]

> "My intention is that the noble deeds of *Dhamma* and the practice of *Dhamma*, which consists of compassion, liberality truthfulness, purity, gentleness and goodness, will thus be promoted among men".

The Asokan Edicts were primarily addressed to the people in general the lay men and lay women. Hence, without referring to the purely Buddhistic terms like the Four Noble Truths, the Noble Eiqhtfold path and Nirvāṇa, Asoka lists in simple language the virtues, the path that a lay person ought to follw. And while doing so, he lists the virtues keeping in view the 'layman's code of conduct' as laid down by the Buddha in the *Sigālovada Sutta*[13] (No. 31 of the *Dīgha-Nikāya*). Asoka preaches the ethical discipline the virtue which lead to the attainmnt of happiness in this world and the next. He preached these virtues to all classes of people, both rich and poor, and endeavoured to inculacte the sirit of true *Dhamma* - self-control, purity of thought, compassions, truthfulness and goodness to all. Moral foundation for a nation is a must for material,mental and spiritual rise. And this is what Asoka endcavoured to achiever through *Dhamma*.

There are two forms of meditation. One form is *Samatha*, Calm or development of mental concentration. The other form is *Vipassanā insight*, which was discovered by the Buddha at the time of His Enligtenment. *Vipassanā* means to see things as they really are. It aims at "exposing the truth of impermanency, the suffering, and the unsubatntial nature of all material, mental phenomena of existence".[14] *(anicca, dukkha, anatta). Vipassanā* ultimately leads to the complete libertion of mind, to the realization of the Ultimate Truth.

Asoka nowhre refer to *Vipassanā*, yet it is felt that besides constant emphasis on the virtuous living *(sīla)*, he must have arranged to preach and teach the people the deeper aspects of the *Dhamma*. In the Pillar Edict VII[15] Asoka speaks of 'manifold *Dhamma* instructions' and order his officers to explain the same in detail to the people. His manifold *Dhamma* instructions must have included instructionson practising the *Dhamma* based on *Sīla* (Morality), *Samādhi*, (Meditation - mastery over mind), and *paññā* (Wisdom); the three essential ingredients of the *Vipassanā* meditation. Some indiction of this is available in the selection of the lay people. If we just have a look at the three *suttas* chosen by Asoka from the *Sutta-Nipāta,* it is apparent that all the three *Suttas* recommended by Asoka lay emphasis on meditation. [16]

Even if it is disputed that Asoka's *Dhamma* instructions did not cover the *Vipassanā* technique as such, yet it cannot be denied that the *Dhamma* preached by him was the universal *Dhamma* and was fully inaccord with the spirit of *Vipassanā*. Asoka's *Dhamma* consisted of the virtues of: Kindness (*dayā*), liberality (*dānam*), truthfulness (*satyam*), inner and outer purity (*śaucam*), gentleness (*mārdavam*), saintliness (*sādhutā*), self-control (*smayama*), purity of heart (*bhāvaśuddhi*), gratitude (*Kritajnatā*), firm devotion (*dridhabhakti*), and attachmnt to morality (*dhamma-rati*), Thus it was the *Dhamma* or *Sila, Samādhi* and *Paññā*, that leads one from darkness to light, from passion to dispassion, from turmoil to tranquillity.

Buddha's teachings stand on three pillars --the *Buddha*, the *Dhamma* and the *Saṅgha*. Of these, *Dhamma* has naturally the central position because it is only the practice of *Dhamma* which enables a person to attaain the highest goal. The late Sayagyi U Ba Khin, the great *Vipassanā* Teacher of modern Burma (the country that preserved the *Vipassanā* technique in its pristine purity), says, [17] "There are three gems, the Buddha, the *Dhamma*, and the *Saṅgha*, Of these three gems, the most important is the *Dhamma* because without the *Dhamma*, a Buddha cannot arise"....... "Buddha is what is called the aggregate of the *Dhammakāya*, the embodiment of the *Dhamma*". likewise, Asoka too speaks of his respect for and faith in the Buddha, the *Dhamma* and the *Sangha*, but the all-pervasive force in his inscriptions is '*Dhamma*'. Singificantly enough, Asoka uses the term '*Dhamma*' as many as125 times[18] in his inscriptions. For him, the practice of *Dhamma* was the most vital thing. So he "governed the people according to *Dhamma* administed justice according to *Dhamma*, caused happiness to them according to *Dhamma*, and protected them according to *Dhamma*[19]". Thus the sound of the *Dhamma* drum (*Dhamma-gosa*) reverberated throughout his Empire. In brief,........ Asoka's *Dhamma-Vijaya* consisted "in the expression of goodwill and assurance of territorial intergrity, the frilendly acts of public utility, and advancement of the cause of humanity through piety".

A Vipassanā student cultivates the four Sublime States (*Brahma - Vihāra*) of *Mettā* - Loving - Kindness; *Karuṇā* - Compasson; *Muditā* - Sympathetic Joy; and *Upekkhā* - Equanimity or Evenmindedness. In tune with the *Metta - Bhāvana* or *Maṅgala - maitrī* of the *Vipassanā* tradition, Asoka says,[20] "There is no greater duty for him than doing good to the whole world". (Major Rock Edict VI). The benevolent Asoka goes on to say:[21] "All men are my children. I wish happiness and welfare to all men, as I would wish to my own children". (First Separate Rock Edict- Dhauli Text). For the material welfare of his subjects, Asoka undertook the provision of public works of utiltiy on an unprecedented scale. And influenced by the virtures of *Mettā* and *Karuṇā* Asoka ordered aboiltion of sacrifical slaughter of animls; *samajas* (merry-making of a kind, accompanied by animal fights and feasting with consumption of meat etc); meat diet for the royal household; "tours of pleasure" accompanied by hunting and other similar amusements.

While keen to preach and propagate the marvellous teachings of the Buddha, Asoka showed equal respect for the various religious sects. Even though an ardent follower of the Buddha himself, he asks no one to adopt Buddhism. Similar is the approach of the modern *Vipassanā* teachers. Goenkaji says,[22] "When an Enlightened One teaches *Dhamma*, it is always pure *Dhamma*, free from sectarianism. pure *Dhamma* is universal truṭh. Pure *Dhamma* is good for all, beneficial to all. It is not at all necessary that one should call oneself a Buddhist ....What really matters is one's actual practices of *Dhamma*".

A *Vipassanā* student is reminded time and again during the *Dhamma* discourses that in order to practise true *Dhamma*, he should shun ritualism and avoid useless religious ceremonies According to Asoka also, "the auspicious ceremonies performed on the occasions of illness, the weddings, the birth éct. are trivial and meaningless[23]". By the third entury B.C. the relic - worship or the caitya- worship had come into vogue amongst the followers of the Buddha. Asoka himself is said to have built as many as 84,000 stūpas throughout his Empire, and some of these stūpas had even the sacred relics of the Buddha enshrined in them, yet, signficantly enough, he does not refer to the relic worship or the like in his inscriptions. For, in his view[24] "The quintessence of *Dhamma* consisted in *sīla* or good conduct, and not in creed, rituals, ceremonies or worship".

In sum, the records of Asoka were not to commemorate his military triumph over Kalinga and other secular achievements but they were intended to "convey the lofty message of an enlightened seer for eternal good and hapiness". Asoka wanted the *Dhamma* to illumine the path

of all to Ultimate Goal, *Nirvāṇa,* reaching which one leaves behind all that is *dukkha;* all that is born of *lobha* (greed), *dosa* (hatred), and *moha* (delusion) and all that is rooted in *avijjā* or Ignorance.

Asoka also called *Dhammāsoka* or *Dharmrāja,* "the King of *Dharma*" passed away in 232 B.C. but respect for *Dhamma* propagated by him endured for a long time. For centuries "the follwers of the Buddha's teaching have called their faith simply *Dharma*[25] or at the most '*Sadharma*' and to have styled themselves as '*Dharmin*' or '*Sadharmin*'".

References

1. H.G. Wells, The Outline History of the World p. 402.

2. Minor Rock Edict I, Maski (Andhra Pradesh) and Gujarra (Madhya Pradesh) texts. cf. D.C. Sircar, *Inscriptions of Asoka*, pp.34-35.

3. D. C. Sircar, op.cit Minor Rock Edict I, p.33. This edict has been found at Sahasaram (Bihar),Ahroura (U.P.) Bairat (Rajasthan), Bahapur (Delhi), Rupnath, Gujara (Madhya Pradesh), Brahmagirl, Jaitinga-Ramesvara, Siddhapura (Karnataka) and Maski, Yerragudi Gavimath, Palkigundu, Rajula-Mandagiri (Andhra Pradesh).

4. D.C. Sircar, op. cit Minor Rock Edict III, p. 38.

5. Sircar translates the sevsen texts listed by Asoka as under: the Exaltation of Disclpline; the Nobel State of Living; the Fears to Come; the Song of the Hermit; the Discourse on the State of a Hermit; the Questions of Upatishya; and the Exhortation to Rahula, which was delivered by the text with the following texts in the Tipitaka:

   Vinaya-samukase - *Vinaya-samukkansa* - "select passages from Vinaya". Cf. *Atthavasavagga* in the *Aṅgutara-Nikāya*, vol.1 pp.98-100.

   Aliya-vasani - *Ariya-vasa (dasa)* "The excellent state of mind", *Digha-Nikaya*, Vol. III, pp. 269, 291; *Aṅguttara-Nikaya*, p.29

   291; *Aṅguttara-Nikāya*, vol. IV p. 29.

   Anagata-bhayani (pañca), Aṅguttara Nikāya, Vol.III.

pp.100-110. *Muni-gata- Muni-sutta, Sutta Nipatā,* 1.12. *(sutta). Moneya-sutta - Nalnka-sutta, Ibid.,* IV, p.16.

Laghulovade - Rahulovade, "Instruction to Rahula', cf. *Ambalatthika - Rahalovāda-sutta, Majjhima Nikāya,* vol. 1. pp.414-20 cf. Sujitkumar Mukhopadhyaya. The Aśokavadāna, Sahitya Akademi, Appendix B. Asoka Inscription, p.154.

6. Romila Thapar, *Asoka and the Decline of the Mauryas.* Appedix V, A Translation of the Edicts of Asoka, p 262.
7. R. K. Mookerji, *Asoka* pp. 61-62.
8. Romila Thapar, op cit. 3rd Major Rock Edict, p.251.
9. Ibid., 4th Major Edct, p. 251.
10. Ibid., 6th Major Edict, pp 254-255.
11. D.C. Sircar, op cit. Pillar Edict II, p.68.
12. Ibid., Pillar Edict VII, pp. 75-76.
13. The six sets of reciprocal duties enumeratd in the *Sigālovāda-suttā,* No. 31 of *Dīgha-nikāya,* are: between parents and children; betwen pupil and teachers; betwen husband and wife; friends and companions; masters and servants; and lastly the laity and Saṅgha. In each case, there are five duties, except in the case of *Saṅgha's* duties to householders, which are six.
14. Nyanatiloka, Buddhist Dictionary - Manual of Buddhist Terms and Discourses p.245.
15. Sujitkumar Mukhopadhyaya, op.cit. Appendix B, *Asoka Inscriptions,* Pillar Edict VII, p. 147.
16. The following three verses are taken from "V, fausboll *Sutta-Nipāta.*"

6. The man who has the strength of understanding

is endowed with virtue and (holy) works, is composed, delights in meditation, is thoughtful, free from ties, free from harshness, and free from passion, him the wise style a Muni"'.(211) ...1.12- *Muni Sutta*, p. 34.

"31, Applying himself to meditation, and being wise, let him find his pleasure in the outskirts of the wood, let him meditate at the root of a tree enjoying himself"'.(709) —III. 11. *Nālaka Sutta,* p. 129.

"18. Let him be with downcast eyes, and not prying, devoted to meditation, very watchful; having acquired equanimity let him with a composed mind cut off the seat of doubt, and misbehaviour".(972). — IV.16 *Sariputta sutta,* p.82.

17. *Vipassanā Journal,* Special Number, 19th January 1983, Hýderabad, Sayings of Sayagyl, last page.

18. The term "*Dhamma*" is used by Asoka 57 times in the 14 Major Rock Edicts and 48 Times in the 7 Major Rock Edicts, and 20 times in other inscriptions.

19. D.C. Sircar, op.cit. Pillar Edict I, p. 67.

20. B. M. Barua, *Asoka and His Inscriptions,* Major Rock Edict VI p. 246.

21. D. C. Sircar op.cit. Rock Edicts XV and XVI, pp. 56 and 59.

22. *Vipassanā, Journal,* Special Number, January 1983, opposite page 67.

23. D. C. Sircar, op.cit. Rock Edict IX, p. 47.

24. Amulyachandra Sen, *Asoka's Edicts,* p. 34.

25. N.N. Vasu, *Modern Buddhism and its Followers in Orissa*, 1911, pp 150-151. Some Buddhists of Orissa (Kalinga still call themselves as "Mahima-Dharmis" or followers of the Praise-worthy Dharma.

XVI

Vipassanā - a Distinct Contribution of Buddhism to World Culture.

Angraj Chaudhary

"Indian culture abroad" is a very intriguing subject on whih volumes have been written and still be written, because there are many ingredients of culture which travelled from Inida to different neighbouring countries and struck their roots there. These include all aspects of life, social, political, religious and spiritual and they range from the gressest to the subtlest. We all know that the message of Buddha was carried alive from this country and elements of Buddhism planted into the hearts of the people of a particular country to cater to their spiritual needs. The ennobling effects of his massage can still be seen in the way of life of a country where Buddism is a living religion.

In this paper I will talk about the *vipassanā* form of meditation and the great influence it has exercised on the minds of the Burmese people. Why I have taken up *vipassanā* to talk about will be at once clear from what I say below. This form of meditation which disappeared from the land of its origin has been in practise in Burma without any interrpution over the centuries and it has been brought back to India in its pristine form in the recent past. This form of meditation which Buddha practised to put an end to sufferings of all kinds such as physical, mental and cosmic, is a distinct contribution made by the Budhha to world culture. It is also a great contribution by Indian missionaries to Burmese culture. Once this form of meditation was taken to Burma by Indian monk missionaries it was learnt by

Burmese monks. It struck its root, had its luxuriant growth and became a part and parcel of the way of life not only of monks but also of the lay people at large.

It is really a matter of great happiness that what was once taught by India to Burma is being learnt by her in this century, Vipassanā ācarya Sri Satya Narayan Goenaka-a Burmese citizen of Indian origin, has brought back this form of meditation from Burma and has been trying to make it popular for the last several years. His yeoman's services can be compared with those of Ācarya Buddhaghosa who translated the whole *Pāli Aṭṭhakathās* back into *Pāli* from Sihali and thus brought back our forgotten treasure.

We may feel proud to know that the *vipassanā* form of meditation is a distinct contribution to world culture, particularly , in the field of yoga, by one of the brilliant sons of India but it is also nonetheless a matter of pride to realise that this form of meditation was preserved in its original form by the Burmese people and they have returned the spiritual heirloom to us without damaging it in any form. *Vipssanā* is now, as ever has been, woven into the pattern of life of the Burmese people.

Let me explain here in brief what *vipassanā* is. Then only we shall be able to assess its quantum of influence in our life and the role it plays in purifying our life. The word *vipassanā* is composed of prefix *vi* and root *pas* which means to see, *Vipassanā* thus means seeing in a special manner. If one practises *vipassanā* he develops special powers in him to see things as they are without reacting to them which we do in ignorance. By practising *vipassanā* we develop *prajñā* insinght) with which the real nature of things develop, (non-attachment) ands purify our mind whigh is polluted by our headed desire for the various objects of the world.

The importance of *vipassanā* can be seen if we know the nature of our mind. It is fickle and unsteady, according to Buddha.

Phandanaṁ capalaṁ cilttaṁ durakkhan dunnivarayam/

Ujum karoti medhāvi usukārova tejanaṁ.

"As a fletcher makes straight his arrow, so does the man make straight the mind, which trembling and unsteady is difficult to guard and restrain". Our unsteady mind keeps on roaming from one object to anothr and thus amasses sensations which cause *taṇhā* (desires) and bind us to the wheel of birth and death, causing immeasurable suffesring to us.

Buddha taught us a way out of suffering. If we can stop fending for our senses we can go a long way in reducing our desires which form the seeds of our rebirth. Mind has got to be controlled. But how can we do so? By practising four *Saṭṭipatthāns.* viz. *kayānupassanā; vedanānupassanā* which helps us in developing awareness of all the states of body, of different kinds of feelings, of our consciousness and also of the various principles of *dhamma*. Thus *vipassanā* does not only help us in keeping an alert and watchful eye on all the sense doors through which sensations keep on pouring in our mind and make us crave for them which in turn cause our suffering but also enable us to penetrate into the conceptions like *santati pannñāti* (conception of series), *ghana pannati* (conception of solidity), *puggala paññati* (conception of personality) and so on. Gradually we realize the ultimate truth and come to know that matter is nothing but a mass of vibrations by observing the physics and chemistry of our body. We realize that all *dhammas* are in a constant state of flux and they are characterized by *anicca* (impermanence, *dukkha* (suffering) and *anatta* (non-substance i. e. no soul theory. That is why Buddha has said explicitly that the only way to purify oneself and put an end to all kinds of sufferings, to achieve insight and to realize *Nibbāna* is to practise four *Sattipatthānas* i.e. *vipassanā*.

Ekāyanoayam Bhikkhave, maggo sattānam visuddhiyā, soksparidevānam samatikkamāya dukkha domanassānaṁ aṭṭhaṁgamāya, ñānasa adhigamāya, nibbānasa sacchikiriyāya, yadidaṁ cattāro satipaṭṭhānā. How do we practise it ? In the beginning a moral foundation is laid. The practitioner takes a vow to abstain from killing, stealing, sexual misconduct, lying. and using intxicants. In a ten day workshop concentrtion is sharpened during the first three days through sustained observation of our breath going in and coming out which in the words of Acāryā S. N. Goenka provides "a bridge between the known and the unknown'. First of all we take a small area below our nostril and observe pressure, pain, lightness, numbness, tingling sensation, heat cold etc. We see them clearly as we acquire concentration of our body. This has two advantages. First, we realize the true nature of *dhanmas* and secondly we succeed in yoking our mind to our breath so that it may not wander uncontrolled. A wandering and roaming mind must of necessity bring in a large number of sensations which cause desires in us. The third that comes a little later when insight dawns on us is that we observe whatever happens in our mind and body without reacting to them. In ordinary life when we lose our temper our brows are arched,our fists ar closed, our teeth are set, our eyes become red and we are full of tensions. A chain of reactions set in causing us incalculable harm. All of this can be stopped if we develop equanimity through *Vipassanā.*

Although *Vipassanā* — the technique of purifying mind and realizing *Nibbāna*, has been discovered and taught by Buddha, it can be practised by followers of all religions because the subject of meditation according to it, is human breath common to all hmanity and the vow that one has to take for a moral foundation includes codes of conduct common to all religions.

It is for this reason that Buddha called his *dhamma* explicit and ciearly explined. He says that it is a *dhamma* which produces results here and now.

"*Svākkāto Bhagavatā dhammo, sanditthiko, akaliko, ehipassiko, epaneyyāko, paccatta veditabbo, viññuhi ti.*"

This unique technique of purifying oneself was completely forgotten in India. Its re-introduction to the land of its origin has a very interesting story. Sri S.N. Goenka a business magnet of Burma suffered terribly from migrain and had to use morphine to kill the pain he suffered from but that also he could do temporarily. He consulted practically all the best doctors of the world, spent a huge amount of money but he was not cured. Then he was advised by one of his friends to go to U-Ba Khin- a *Vipassanācarya* who also worked as Accountant General in Burma. U-Ba Khin taught him to practise *Vipassanā* which had a mirculous effect on him. The monstrous migrain was gone. He was then convinced of the efficacy of this form of meditastion. Setting aside his material business of crores of rupess, he took to the spiritual business of imparting this technique to all people belonging to all races and religions and it is he who brought this technique from Burma to India in its pristine form. *Vipassanā* (insight medtation) goes a long way in removing the heaps of impuritie dumped in our mind in our serveral previous lives due to our own actions and frees us of our mental tensions and cures us of our psycho-somatic diseases. In the words of *Vipassanacarya* Goenka, "meditation is an art of living. We must train our minds not to run away from problems but to go to the depths, to find their causes and then eradicate them. The mind has accumulted so much negativity -anger, hatred, aversion, fear, jealousy and passions. We have to free ourselves of these."

Meditation camps are held in jails also. Criminals have practised it and the results have been wonderful. They feel changed and wish to live a pure life.

This form of meditation can be practised any where and every where in all situations of life and anybody can practise it. Its growing popularity is an indication of the fact that *Vipassanā* is a distinct contribution of Buddhism to world culture.

As far as Burma is concerned, *vipassanā* has deeply affected the life of Burmese people, so much so that training in *Vipassanā* even for a short while is regarded as essential for all people working in office or elsewhere. It has become a way of life.

Bibliography

A.C. Taylor (Ed.) *Patisambhimagga* Pali Text Society. Vol. I, 1905, Vol. II, 1907

Alex Wayman, *Buddhist Insight* Motilal Banarsi Das, Delhi

Amulya Chandra Sen, *Asoka's Edicts* Calcutta, 1956.

Ādi Grantha (Holy Book of the Sikhs) Sri Dadami Bir; various editions; standard pagination 1430.

B.C. Law *A Designation of Human Types* (Translation of Puggalapaññatti), Pali Text Society. 1922 (Reprint 1979)

Bahadur Mal, *Religion of Buddha*, Vishveshvaranda Publication, Hoshiarpur

Bhikkhu Jagdish Kashyap (Ed.) *Digha Nikāya* Pali Publication Board, Nalanda, 1960

— (Ed.) *Vināya Pitaka (Mahāvagga)*

Pali Publication Board, Nalanda, 19€0

— (Ed.) *Aṅguttara Nikāya*

Pali Publication Board, Nalanda, 1960

— (Ed.) *Patisambhidāmagga*

Pali Publication Board, Nalanda, 1960

— (Ed.) *Paṭṭhānapakarṇa*

Pali Publication Board, Nalanda, 1960

— (Ed.) *Khuddaka Nikāya*

Pali publication Board, Nalanda, 1960

— (Ed.) *Saṃyutta Nikāya*

Pali Publication Board, Nalanda, 1960.

— (Ed.) *Dhammasaṅgani*

Pali Publication Board, Nalanda, 1960

— (Ed.) *Vibhanga*

Pali Publication Board, Nalanda, 1960

Bhikkhu Nyanmoli *The Path of Purification* (Translation of *Visuddhimagga*) Buddhist Publication Society. Kandy, Sri Lanka, Fourth edition, 1979 (First edition, 1953)

B.M. Barua, *Aśoka and his Inscriptions* New Age Publications, Calcutta, 1968. (edition)

C.A.F. Rhys Davids (trs.) *Psalms of the Early Buddhists: Psalms of the Sisters* (Translation of Therigāthā) Pali Text Society, 1980 (First published in 1909)

— (trs.) *Buddhist Psychological Ethics* (Translations of *Dhammasaṅgani*) Pali Text Society. 1974 (3rd Edition)

D.C. Circar *Inscriptions of Aśoka* Publications Division, Govt. of India, New Delhi, 1976.

D.D. Kosambi (Ed.) *Visuddhimagga* Bhartya Bhavan, Bombay, 1940

— (Ed.) *Abhidhammatthasaṅgaho*, 1940

Dwarka Das Shastri, (Ed.), *Milindapañhapali* Baudha Bharti, Varanasi 1971.

— (Ed.) *Visuddhimagga*, Baudha Bharti, Varanasi, 1977.

Edward Conze, *Buddhist Meditation*, Harper Torch Books, New York, 1956.

F.L. Woodward (trs.) *The Kindered Sayings* (Translation of *Samyutta Nikāya*) Pali Text Society, 1979 (First edition, 1930).

— Yogāvacara's Manual Pali Text Society, 1916 (Reprint 1982)

Henepola Gunaratana, *The Path of Serenity and Insight* Motilal Banarsi Das, Delhi, 1985.

H.G. Wells, Outline *History of the World* Arihant, Jaipur (2 vols.) 1989.

I.B. Horner (trs.) *The Middle Length Sayings* (Translation of *Majjhima Nikāya*) Pali Text Soceity, Ist Vol. 1976 2nd impression, (Ist Impression in 1954).

James Strachey (Gen Ed.) *The Complete Psychological Works of Sigmund Freud* The Hogarth Press, London. Vol. VII 1975. (First published in 1953)

J.L. Shastri (Ed.) *Ancient Indian Tradition and Mythology: Siva-Purāna (Satarudra Samhita)* Moti Lal Banarsi Das, Delhi, Vol. II, Part II

John Walters, *Mind Unshaken,* Ridder and Co. London..

Lord Chalmers. (trs.) *Further Dialogues of the Buddha* (Translation of *Majjhima Nikāya*) Humphrey Milford London Vol. II 1927.

Mahesh Tiwary (Ed.) *Puggala-Paññatti Aṭṭhakathā* Nav Nalanda Mahavihar Nalanda. 1968.

— (Ed.) *Sumaṅgala Vilasini (Dīgha Nikāya Aṭṭhakathā)* Nav Nalanda Mahavihar, Nalanda 3 Vol.

— (Ed.) *Paṭṭhāna Aṭṭhakathā* Nalanda Mahavihar, Nalanda, 1972.

Maurice Winternitz, *History of Indian Literature* Orient Books, Reprint Corpn; New Delhi, 1979.

Narada Mahathera, (trs.) *Dhammapada* (Text and Translation) Mahabodhi Society Of India, Calcutta 1943.

Nina Gorkan. *Buddhism in Daily Life* Dhamma Study Group, Bangkok.

N.N. Vasu, *Modern Buddhism— Its Followers in Orissa.* Gian Publishers, Delhi 1986.

Nyantiloka, *Buddhist Dictionary*—Manual of Buddhist Terms and Discousses. Buddhist Publication Society, Kandy, Sri Lanka 1980 (4th Edition).

P.V. Bapat and R.D. Vadekar (Edts.) *Aṭṭhasālini* Poona. 1942

— (Ed.) *Dhammasaṅgani* Poona, 1940.

R.D. Vadekar (Ed.) *Milinda-Pañha* Bombay University Publication Bombay. 1943.

Revatadhamma (Ed.) *Visuddhimagga* Varanaseya Sanskrit Vishwavidalaya, Varanasi 1969.

— and R.S. Tripathi, *Abhidhammathasaṅgaho* Sanskrit University, Varanasi 1967.

R. Morris (Ed.) *Aṅguttara Nikāya* Pali Text Society Vol. II 1888 Revised Reprint 1976.

Romila Thapar, *Aśoka and the Decline of Mauryas* Oxford University Press, Delhi. 1985

Sujit Kumar Mukhpadhyaya, *The Aśokavādana* Sahitya Akademy, New Delhi 1963.

T.A. Gopinath Rao, *Elements of Hindu Iconography* Paragan Book Reprint Corpn, New York Vol. II. Part I (Reprint of 1914 edition)

Tepsiddhi Muni Mahāthera, *Path to Nibbāna* Vipassana Meditation Centre Bangkok.

T.W. Rhys Davids (Ed.) *Yogāvacara Manual* Pali Text Society. 1896 (Reprint 1981)

T.W. and C.A.F. Rhys Davids (trs.) *Dialogues of the Buddha* (Translation of *Dīgha Nikāya*) Sacred Books of the Buddhists Henry Frowde, London (Oxford University Press) Vol. III. Part I. 1910

T.W. Rhys Davids and Hermann Oldenberg, (trs.) *Vinay Texts* Sacred Books of the East Series, Motilal Banarsi Das, Delhi Part III, 1965.

T.W. Rhys Davids and J.E. Carpenter (Edts.) *Sumṅgala Vilāsini Dīgha Nikāya Aṭṭhakathā Pali Text Society vol. I, 1886.*

T.W. Rhys Davids and J.E. Carpenter (Edts.) *Dīgha Nikāya* Pali Text Society. Vol. I 1989 (Reprint 1975); Vol.II 1903 (Reprint 1982); Vol. III 1910 (Reprint 1976).

— and William Stede, *Pali English Dictionary*, Pali Text Society, 1959.

Fausboll (trs.) *Sutta Nipāta* Sacred Books of the East Series. Motilal Banarsi Das, Delhi Vol. X, Part II, 1973.

Vipassanā Journal Special Number, Hyderabad (Sayings of Sayaji)

V. Trencker (Ed.) *Majjhima Nikāya* Pali Text Soceity Vol. I. 1888.

*****

General Index

A

D

E

F

G

H

I

J

O

P

R

T